Cambridge
Key English Test
3

WITH ANSWERS

Examination papers from University of Cambridge ESOL Examinations: English for Speakers of Other Languages

CAMBRIDGE UNIVERSITY PRESS
Cambridge, New York, Melbourne, Madrid, Cape Town,
Singapore, São Paulo, Delhi, Tokyo, Mexico City

Cambridge University Press
The Edinburgh Building, Cambridge CB2 8RU, UK

www.cambridge.org
Information on this title: www.cambridge.org/9780521754798

First published 2003
10th printing 2011

Printed in the United Kingdom at the University Press, Cambridge

A catalogue record for this publication is available from the British Library

ISBN 978-0-521-75479-8 Student's Book with Answers
ISBN 978-0-521-75478-1 Student's Book
ISBN 978-0-521-75480-4 Teacher's Book
ISBN 978-0-521-75482-8 Audio CD
ISBN 978-0-521-75481-1 Audio Cassette

Cambridge University Press has no responsibility for the persistence or
accuracy of URLs for external or third-party internet websites referred to in
this publication, and does not guarantee that any content on such websites is,
or will remain, accurate or appropriate. Information regarding prices, travel
timetables and other factual information given in this work is correct at
the time of first printing but Cambridge University Press does not guarantee
the accuracy of such information thereafter.

Page makeup and book design by Oxford Designers & Illustrators

Contents

Acknowledgements

The publishers are grateful for permission to reproduce copyright material. It has not always been possible to identify the sources of all the material used, and in such cases the publishers would welcome information from the copyright owners.

Illustrations by David Eaton

Book design by Peter Ducker MSTD

Cover design by Dunne & Scully

The cassette/CD which accompanies this book was recorded at Studio AVP, London.

To the student

This book is for students preparing for the University of Cambridge ESOL Examinations Key English Test (KET). It contains four complete tests based on the new test format from March 2004.

What is KET?

KET is an examination for students of English as a foreign language. It tests Reading, Writing, Listening and Speaking. The KET examination is at Cambridge Level One (Council of Europe Level A2).

Paper 1	1 hour 10 minutes	**Reading and Writing**	9 parts	50% of total marks
Paper 2	about 30 minutes	**Listening**	5 parts	25% of total marks
Paper 3	8–10 minutes	**Speaking**	2 parts	25% of total marks

How do I prepare for KET?

It is important to know what type of questions are in the KET examination. Doing the tests in this book will help you. Practise putting your answers on the sample answer sheets on pages 126–128 (you may photocopy these pages). This will help you to understand what you have to do in the real test.

Reading: Read some books in simple English from your library or local bookshop. Try to guess the words you don't know before you use a dictionary to check them. Also, use an English learner's dictionary when you study. If you live in a tourist area, there may be some signs or notices in English outside restaurants and shops or in railway stations and airports. Read these and try to understand them.

Writing: Write short letters or messages in English to a friend who is learning English with you or find an English-speaking pen-friend to write to. Write about your daily life (your home, work or school and your family). If you go on holiday, write postcards in English and send them to your English-speaking friends.

Listening: Listen to the cassettes that come with English course books so you can hear different people speaking English. Watch English-language programmes on television and listen to English on the radio if possible.

Speaking: Talk in English with friends who are studying with you. Ask each other questions about your daily lives, your future plans and about other towns, countries or places you have visited.

We hope this book helps you when you take the KET examination. Good luck!

Test 1

PAPER 1   READING AND WRITING (1 hour 10 minutes)

PART 1
QUESTIONS 1–5

Which notice (A–H) says this (1–5)?
For questions 1–5, mark the correct letter A–H on the answer sheet.

EXAMPLE	ANSWER
0 We work fast.	**H**

1   This is not for adults.

2   You can't drive this way.

3   We can help you day and night.

4   You can have dinner here.

5   Come here to book a holiday.

A
> YOUTH CLUB
> Under 16s only

B
> *Half-price drinks
> with 3-course meals!*

C
> CITY CENTRE
> CLOSED TO TRAFFIC
> ALL DAY TODAY

D
> *Tourist Information
> open 24 hours*

E
> NO PETROL STATION
> ON MOTORWAY

F
> TURNER TRAVEL
> *Fly away to the sun
> this summer*

G
> SCHOOL OFFICE
> CLOSED FOR LUNCH

H
> We repair shoes **QUICKLY**
> 8 a.m. – 5 p.m.

PART 2

QUESTIONS 6–10

Read the sentences (6–10) about Sam's new computer.
Choose the best word (A, B or C) for each space.
For questions 6–10, mark A, B or C on the answer sheet.

EXAMPLE	ANSWER
0 Sam's father .... him a new computer for his birthday.	**A**
A bought **B** paid **C** spent	

6 He .... Sam how to use it.

   A learnt   **B** showed   **C** studied

7 Sam sent an e-mail .... to his friend Billy to tell him about his nice present.

   A message   **B** programme   **C** form

8 Billy came to Sam's house and they did their geography .... together.

   A subject   **B** homework   **C** class

9 They were .... because they found some information about rivers on the internet.

   A happy   **B** interesting   **C** pleasant

10 Afterwards, they .... playing a new computer game together.

   A wanted   **B** thanked   **C** enjoyed

PART 3

QUESTIONS 11–15

Complete the five conversations.

For questions 11–15, mark A, B or C on the answer sheet.

EXAMPLE		ANSWER
Where do you come from?	A New York. B School. C Home.	A

11 Who's that man with the green sweater?
- (A) He's my brother.
- (B) It's John's.
- (C) I don't know it.

12 Where's Amanda gone?
- (A) She's at the station.
- (B) She'll arrive tomorrow.
- (C) She's going to leave tonight.

13 I hate shopping.
- (A) So do I.
- (B) Certainly.
- (C) That's all right.

14 How long did the journey take?
- (A) About 500 kilometres.
- (B) Almost 5 hours.
- (C) Last week.

15 The room costs £55 a night.
- (A) I don't take it.
- (B) Give me two, please.
- (C) That's a lot.

QUESTIONS 16–20

Complete the conversation in a garage.

What does David say to the mechanic?

For questions 16–20, mark the correct letter A–H on the answer sheet.

EXAMPLE	ANSWER
Mechanic: Good morning. How can I help you?	
David: **0**	E

Mechanic:	Certainly. What's the problem?	**A**	Oh dear. Can you repair it now?
David:	**16**		
		B	That will be fine.
Mechanic:	How long have you had the car?		
David:	**17**	**C**	Thanks. How much will it cost?
Mechanic:	Hm, there may be something wrong with the engine.	**D**	It's only Monday today. I'll go to another garage.
David:	**18**		
Mechanic:	I'm afraid we have a lot of work at the moment. I can't do it until Friday.	**E**	Would you have a look at my car, please?
David:	**19**	**F**	I bought it new about four years ago.
Mechanic:	Well, I suppose I can do it on Wednesday.		
David:	**20**	**G**	It goes at eighty kilometres an hour.
Mechanic:	Bring it in at 8.30 in the morning.		
		H	It won't start in the morning.

PART 4

QUESTIONS 21–27

Read the article about Howard Bonnier.

Are sentences 21–27 'Right' (A) or 'Wrong' (B)?

If there is not enough information to answer 'Right' (A) or 'Wrong' (B), choose 'Doesn't say' (C).

For questions 21–27, mark A, B or C on the answer sheet.

HOWARD BONNIER

Bray is a beautiful village about fifty kilometres west of London. A young Englishman named Howard Bonnier opened a restaurant called *The Palace* there about three and a half months ago. Not many people in Britain know Mr Bonnier's name yet, but he's already quite famous in France. This is because he has written in French magazines about almost all the best restaurants in that country. He's only 29 years old.

When Howard was a teenager, he often went to restaurants with his mother and father. He liked doing this so much that he decided not to buy lots of clothes and CDs; instead, he used his money to visit France and eat in good restaurants. He also bought a lot of French and English cookbooks – he says he has more than two hundred and fifty!

So why did he decide to open a restaurant? Simply because he loves cooking. Has it been an easy thing to do? He says it's expensive to start your own restaurant and it's much more difficult to cook for fifty people than to cook for your family, but he's sure he's done the right thing.

EXAMPLE	ANSWER
0 Howard is French.	**B**
A Right **B** Wrong **C** Doesn't say	

21   *The Palace* has been open for less than a year.

    A Right   **B** Wrong   **C** Doesn't say

22   Lots of people in France know about Howard.

    A Right   **B** Wrong   **C** Doesn't say

23   Howard's parents took him out to restaurants.

    A Right   **B** Wrong   **C** Doesn't say

24   Howard has always spent a lot of money on clothes.

    A Right   **B** Wrong   **C** Doesn't say

25   Howard has written books about French cooking.

    A Right   **B** Wrong   **C** Doesn't say

26   It costs a lot of money to eat in Howard's restaurant.

    A Right   **B** Wrong   **C** Doesn't say

27   Howard says cooking for a lot of people is easy.

    A Right   **B** Wrong   **C** Doesn't say

PART 5

QUESTIONS 28–35

Read the article about line dancing.

Choose the best word (A, B or C) for each space (28–35).

For questions 28–35, mark A, B or C on the answer sheet.

Line dancing

Thousands of people in Britain ....**0**........ a new
hobby – line dancing. In almost ....**28**........ town, you
will find clubs and classes for this new activity.

'Line dancing is easy to learn. If you have two feet and can walk, then you can do
it!' Fiona Lever, a teacher, ...**29**........ . 'You don't need a partner because you dance
........**30**........ groups. It's the ....**31**........ way to make new friends. In my classes, ...**32**........
are young and old people. The boys like it because they can make a lot of noise with
their feet ....**33**........ the dances!'

When ....**34**........ line dancing begin? Most people think it started about fifteen years
........**35**........ when American country music became famous in Britain.

EXAMPLE			ANSWER
0 A have	**B** had	**C** having	**A**

28 A all	**B** some	**C** every	
29 A say	**B** says	**C** saying	
30 A at	**B** to	**C** in	
31 A best	**B** better	**C** good	
32 A here	**B** there	**C** they	
33 A among	**B** across	**C** during	
34 A has	**B** is	**C** did	
35 A after	**B** ago	**C** since	

PART 6

QUESTIONS 36–40

Read the descriptions (36–40) of some things you may find in your bag.

What is the word for each description?

The first letter is already there. There is one space for each other letter in the word.

For questions 36–40, write the words on the answer sheet.

EXAMPLE	ANSWER
0 You use this to write with.	p _e_ _n_

36 If you lose this, you won't be able to get into your house. k _ _

37 Many people put these on when they want to read something. g _ _ _ _ _ _

38 People pay for things with this. m _ _ _ _

39 If it has been windy, you may need to do your hair with this. c _ _ _

40 You write important dates in this so you don't forget them. d _ _ _ _ _

PART 7

QUESTIONS 41–50

Complete this letter.
Write ONE word for each space (41–50).
For questions 41–50, write your words on the answer sheet.

Dear Lynne and Tony,

I'm writing (**Example:** ....) say thank you ....**41**.... the two nights I stayed in ....**42**.... lovely home. It ....**43**.... good to see you again.

Here ....**44**.... the photographs ....**45**.... your children that you asked for. They're good photos, aren't ....**46**.... ? I hope you like ....**47**.... . I really love my new camera.

I ....**48**.... going to visit my sister in New York next week. I ....**49**.... take a lot of photos there, too. I haven't seen my sister for a long ....**50**.... .

Thanks again.

Love,

Roy

PART 8

QUESTIONS 51–55

Read the two e-mail messages.

Fill in the information on the visa application form.

For questions 51–55, write the information on the answer sheet.

To:	Churchill Language School, Oxford
From:	Alice Silveiro

I would like to study at your school. I work in the reception of a hotel in my home town, Sao Paulo, Brazil, and English is important for my job.

Where can I stay in Oxford? I shall spend two months in Britain.

Alice Silveiro

To:	Alice Silveiro
From:	Churchill Language School, Oxford

We have six-week courses for people who want to study English. There is a house for students next to the school, in Park Road, at number 26.

You will need a visa.

Churchill Language School

VISA APPLICATION FORM

Name:		*Alice Silveiro*
Nationality:	51	
Job:	52	
Address in Britain:	53	
Why are you visiting Britain?	54	
How long will you stay?	55	

PART 9

QUESTION 56

Read this postcard from your friend, Paul.

POSTCARD

I'm very pleased you're going to visit me on Saturday. How will you get here? What time will you arrive? What shall we do?

See you soon.

Yours,

Paul

Write Paul a postcard. Answer his questions.

Write 25–35 words.

Write your postcard on the answer sheet.

PAPER 2 LISTENING (approximately 30 minutes including 8 minutes transfer time)

PART 1

QUESTIONS 1–5

You will hear five short conversations.
You will hear each conversation twice.
There is one question for each conversation.
For questions 1–5, put a tick ☑ under the right answer.

EXAMPLE

0 How many people were at the meeting?

3	**13**	**30**
A ☐	B ☐	C ☑

---

1 When did Gary start his new job?

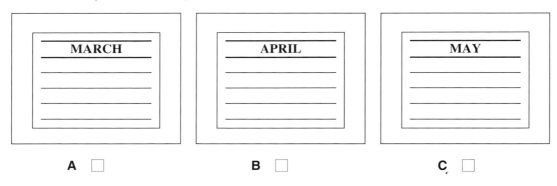

MARCH	APRIL	MAY
A ☐	B ☐	C ☐

2 What time does the film start?

4.30 and 7.00	**4.30 and 7.30**	**4.00 and 7.30**
A ☐	B ☐	C ☐

3   What was the weather like on Saturday?

A ☐   **B** ☐   **C** ☐

4   Which motorway will they take?

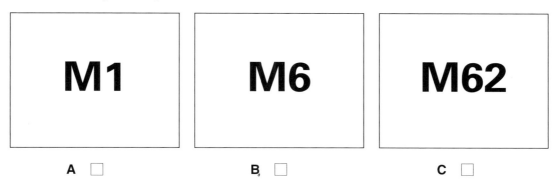

A ☐   **B** ☐   **C** ☐

5   Which book does Lorna want?

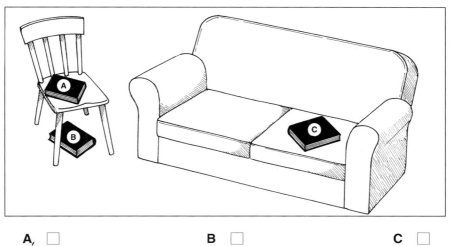

A ☐   **B** ☐   **C** ☐

PART 2

QUESTIONS 6–10

Listen to Sue talking to a friend about her new clothes.

Why did Sue decide to buy each thing?

For questions 6–10, write a letter A–H next to the clothes.

You will hear the conversation twice.

EXAMPLE

0   jeans   **F**

CLOTHES SUE BOUGHT

6   jacket   ☐

7   dress   ☐

8   sweater   ☐

9   coat   ☐

10 t-shirt   ☐

WHY?

A   big

B   cheap

C   expensive

D   light

E   long

F   purple

G   short

H   soft

PART 3

QUESTIONS 11–15

Listen to Jan talking to Steve about getting a student travel card.

For questions 11–15, tick ☑ A, B or C.

You will hear the conversation twice.

EXAMPLE		ANSWER
0 How is Steve going to go to London?		
A by bus		☐
B by car		☐
C by train		☑

11   How much is a travel card?

    A   £6   ☐

    B   £16   ☐

    C   £60   ☐

12   Jan will need

    A   one photo.   ☐

    B   two photos.   ☐

    C   four photos.   ☐

13   Photos are less expensive

    A   in the photographer's shop.   ☐

    B   in the library.   ☐

    C   in the post office.   ☐

14 For the travel card, Jan must take

   A   a letter.   ☐

   B   her passport.   ☐

   C   her driving licence.   ☐

15 Jan can get a travel card from

   A   her college.   ☐

   B   the travel agent's.   ☐

   C   the tourist office.   ☐

PART 4

QUESTIONS 16–20

You will hear a man speaking on the telephone.
Listen and complete questions 16–20.
You will hear the conversation twice.

TELEPHONE MESSAGE

To: Mr Brown

From: **16** David GRAHAM

Not in school because he has: **17** a bad BACK

Students should read pages: **18**   58   to   73

David will return to school on: **19** TUESDAY   afternoon

                            at: **20** 2:45   p.m.

PART 5

QUESTIONS 21–25

You will hear some information about a pop concert.
Listen and complete questions 21–25.
You will hear the information twice.

POP CONCERT

Name of group:		Red River
In London:	From:	October 28th
	To:	**21** November 2nd.
Price of ticket:		**22** £ 37 each
Telephone no:		**23** 283 0065
Place:		**24** South _____ Bank Hall
	In:	**25** TRINITY _____ Street

You now have 8 minutes to write your answers on the answer sheet.

PAPER 3   SPEAKING (8–10 minutes)

The Speaking test lasts 8 to 10 minutes. You will take the test with another candidate. There are two examiners, but only one of them will talk to you. The examiner will ask you questions and ask you to talk to the other candidate.

Part 1 (5–6 minutes)

The examiner will ask you and your partner some questions. These questions will be about your daily life, past experience and future plans. For example, you may have to speak about your school, job, hobbies or home town.

Part 2 (3–4 minutes)

You and your partner will speak to each other. You will ask and answer questions. The examiner will give you a card with some information on it. The examiner will give your partner a card with some words on it. Your partner will use the words on the card to ask you questions about the information you have. Then you will change roles.

Test 2

PAPER 1 READING AND WRITING (1 hour 10 minutes)

PART 1

QUESTIONS 1–5

Which notice (A–H) says this (1–5)?
For questions 1–5, mark the correct letter A–H on the answer sheet.

EXAMPLE	ANSWER
0 You can't come in here.	**D**

1 You can't leave your bicycle here.

2 Adults shouldn't let children play with this.

3 You can buy children's clothes here.

4 Do not come in if you are not wearing the right clothes.

5 Use this door to go outside.

A | School Uniform Department – This floor

B | DANGER!
No hard hat? No boots?
NO ENTRANCE

C | NO BICYCLES AGAINST THIS WINDOW

D | KEEP OUT

E | BICYCLES ONLY

F | Exit to Shoemaker Road

G | DANGER!
KEEP AWAY FROM CHILDREN

H | BICYCLES TO RENT
Adults   £3.50 per hour
Children   £2.00 per hour

PART 2

QUESTIONS 6–10

Read the sentences (6–10) about going to a new school.
Choose the best word (A, B or C) for each space.
For questions 6–10, mark A, B or C on the answer sheet.

EXAMPLE	ANSWER
0 It was the morning of Sally's first ………………… at her new school.	**B**
A moment **B** day **C** hour	

6 Sally felt rather ………………… because she didn't know anybody.

    A unhappy   **B** poor   **C** single

7 The teacher ………………… Sally to the classroom.

    A put   **B** went   **C** took

8 Sally sat next to a girl with blonde ………………… called Amy.

    A eyes   **B** teeth   **C** hair

9 At lunchtime, Amy gave Sally an apple and ………………… her all about the school.

    A told   **B** learned   **C** spoke

10 By the end of the afternoon, Amy was Sally's ………………… friend.

    A lovely   **B** best   **C** excellent

PART 3

QUESTIONS 11–15

Complete the five conversations.

For conversations 11–15, mark A, B or C on the answer sheet.

EXAMPLE

How are you?

A   I'm 18.
B   I'm Sally.
C   I'm fine.

ANSWER

C

11	£500 is too expensive.	A	Not many.
		B	Why not?
		C	I agree.

12	I've got an appointment with my doctor today.	A	How does he feel?
		B	What's the matter with you?
		C	Who do you want?

13	Would you like anything else?	A	That's all, thank you.
		B	Yes, I like everything.
		C	Two, please.

14	When is your mother's birthday?	A	She's thirty-nine.
		B	It was last week.
		C	It's a long time.

15	Shall we go to the shops now?	A	I'm too tired.
		B	They're very good.
		C	Not at all.

QUESTIONS 16–20

Complete the conversation at an airport.

What does Stephen say to the airport assistant?

For questions 16–20, mark the correct letter A–H on the answer sheet.

EXAMPLE		ANSWER
Assistant:	Good morning. Can I see your ticket, please?	
Stephen:	0	**G**

Assistant:	You're going to fly to Scotland?	**A**	Well, I suppose I can get something to eat. Where's the restaurant?
Stephen:	**16**		
Assistant:	I'm sorry, but there's a short delay because of fog.	**B**	Here's my passport.
Stephen:	**17**	**C**	Yes, that's right. I'm going to visit my family.
Assistant:	About an hour. It won't be any more.		
Stephen:	**18**	**D**	By the window, please.
Assistant:	It's on the first floor. Can I take your suitcases now, please?	**E**	Yes, but not this bag. Is it all right to take it on the plane?
Stephen:	**19**	**F**	That's bad news. How long for?
Assistant:	Yes, you can take one piece of luggage with you. Where would you like to sit?	**G**	Yes, here you are.
Stephen:	**20**	**H**	Can I smoke if I sit there?
Assistant:	There you are. Number 24A. Enjoy your trip.		

PART 4

QUESTIONS 21–27

Read the article about a writer.

Are sentences 21–27 'Right' (A) or 'Wrong' (B)?

If there is not enough information to answer 'Right' (A) or 'Wrong' (B), choose 'Doesn't say' (C).

For questions 21–27, mark A, B or C on the answer sheet.

Bill Prince-Smith

Bill Prince-Smith was a farmer and a teacher and a dentist before he became a writer of children's books at the age of 60. Now, thirteen years later, he has written more than 80 books. Every day, he goes into his office and writes. In the evening, he gives the work to his wife to read. 'She tells me when she doesn't like something,' says Bill. 'My ten grandchildren don't live near here but they also read my stories and say if they are good or bad.' And so Bill has learned what young children want to read.

Bill writes about the life in his village and on the farms near it. His fifth book is his favourite: *The Sheepdog* is about a farmer and the dog that helps him. 'I have always liked animals,' says Bill, 'and dogs are so clever, they learn very quickly.'

Last year, the book was made into a film with real animals and actors. The film-makers used the latest computer technology to make people think that the animals are speaking. Bill was very pleased with the film. 'Sometimes film-makers change books, but they didn't change mine and I love the film.'

EXAMPLE	ANSWER
0 Bill Prince-Smith has had several jobs.	**A**
A Right **B** Wrong **C** Doesn't say	

21 Bill became a writer thirteen years ago.

A Right   **B** Wrong   **C** Doesn't say

22 Bill writes his books in the evenings.

A Right   **B** Wrong   **C** Doesn't say

23 Bill shows his writing to his wife.

A Right   **B** Wrong   **C** Doesn't say

24 Bill writes books about his grandchildren.

A Right   **B** Wrong   **C** Doesn't say

25 *The Sheepdog* was Bill's first book.

A Right   **B** Wrong   **C** Doesn't say

26 Bill prefers writing about animals to writing about people.

A Right   **B** Wrong   **C** Doesn't say

27 The film of *The Sheepdog* is different from the book.

A Right   **B** Wrong   **C** Doesn't say

PART 5

QUESTIONS 28–35

Read the article about an animal, the otter.

Choose the best word (A, B or C) for each space (28–35).

For questions 28–35, mark A, B or C on the answer sheet.

Otters

Not many people ....**0**....... seen an otter.
These animals live ......**28**...... rivers and
make their homes from small pieces of
wood. They usually come ......**29**...... of their
homes at night. Otters are very good in the water and can swim at more than
10 kilometres ......**30**...... hour. They have thick brown hair and this ......**31**...... them
warm in the water. An otter can close ......**32**...... ears and nose. This means
otters can stay under water ......**33**...... several minutes.

Twenty years ago, there were ......**34**...... otters in Great Britain. The water in the
rivers was so dirty that many fish and insects died and the otters couldn't find
anything to eat. But today there is lots of food for them ......**35**...... the rivers are
clean again.

EXAMPLE			ANSWER
0 **A** did	**B** have	**C** are	**B**

28 **A** at   **B** near   **C** next

29 **A** away   **B** off   **C** out

30 **A** one   **B** an   **C** a

31 **A** keeps   **B** keep   **C** kept

32 **A** the   **B** their   **C** its

33 **A** since   **B** during   **C** for

34 **A** few   **B** little   **C** any

35 **A** after   **B** because   **C** when

PART 6

QUESTIONS 36–40

Read the descriptions (36–40) of some things you can see when you travel by road.
What is the word for each description?
The first letter is already there. There is one space for each other letter in the word.
For questions 36–40, write the words on the answer sheet.

EXAMPLE	ANSWER
0 You can drive fast here.	m _o_ _t_ _o_ _r_ _w_ _a_ _y_

36 Go here when you need petrol for your car.   g _ _ _ _ _ _

37 This will take you over a river or another road.   b _ _ _ _ _ _

38 You must show this person your driving licence if he asks for it.   p _ _ _ _ _, _ _ _ _ _ _ _

39 You can go left, right or straight on at this place where two roads meet.   c _ _ _ _ _ _ _ _ _

40 If these are red, the traffic has to wait.   l _ _ _ _ _ _

PART 7

QUESTIONS 41–50

Complete these notes.

Write ONE word for each space (41–50).

For questions 41–50, write your words on the answer sheet.

TO ALL STUDENTS:

Would you (**Example:** ....*like*....) to come on a camping trip
.......**41**...... weekend?

We are going to ....**42**...... to the forest in the school bus
and we will stay at a camp-site .....**43**...... Friday to Sunday.
.....**44**..... has hot showers and .....**45**..... small shop and you
.....**46**..... rent bicycles there.

The trip ....**47**...... £25. It is very cold there .....**48**...... night,
so you should take warm clothes and you will ....**49**...... to
wear strong shoes.

.....**50**..... you want to come, tell me today.

Ahmed

Student Secretary

PART 8

QUESTIONS 51–55

Read the advertisement for summer jobs and the e-mail message.

Fill in the summer job application form.

For questions 51–55, write the information on the answer sheet.

GRANTON UNIVERSITY
STUDENT JOBS
AUGUST

Europe Computers:
 Cleaner, start next month.

Mill Farm:
 Fruit pickers, until end of this month

Brown's Hotel:
 Receptionist needed now, for 4 weeks, must speak a foreign language.

| To: | J & S Becker |

Hi Mum and Dad!

My history course finishes on 28 July. I want to find a job for a month where I can practise my French and German and perhaps use a computer. I'll come back home to Canada in September.

Love
Helen

SUMMER JOB APPLICATION FORM

Name: *Helen Becker*

Nationality: **51** ~~_____~~

University course: **52** ~~_____~~

Foreign languages: **53** ~~_____~~

Job wanted at: **54** ~~_____~~

Which month can you work? **55** ~~_____~~

PART 9

QUESTION 56

Read this note from your friend, Chris.

Why didn't you come to the party last night?

Can you meet me on Saturday? What do you want to do?

Chris

Write a note to Chris. Answer the questions.

Write 25–35 words.

Write your note on the answer sheet.

PAPER 2   LISTENING (approximately 30 minutes including 8 minutes transfer time)

PART 1

QUESTIONS 1–5

You will hear five short conversations.

You will hear each conversation twice.

There is one question for each conversation.

For questions 1–5, put a tick ☑ under the right answer.

EXAMPLE

0   How many people were at the meeting?

3	**13**	**30**
A ☐	B ☐	C ☑

1   What colour is Kathy's bedroom now?

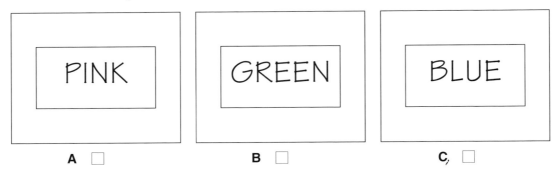

PINK	GREEN	BLUE
A ☐	B ☐	C, ☐

2   Which platform does the woman's train leave from?

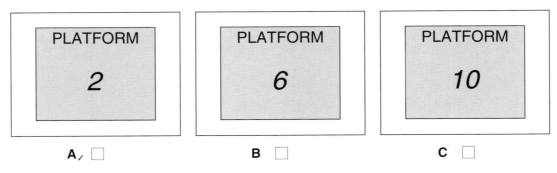

PLATFORM 2	PLATFORM 6	PLATFORM 10
A, ☐	B ☐	C ☐

3   How is Susan going to get to the airport?

      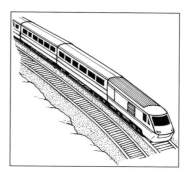

A, ☐   B ☐   C ☐

4   Which is Anna's family?

A ☐   B, ☐   C ☐

5   When is Kim's birthday party?

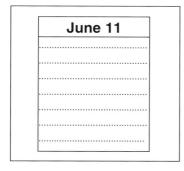   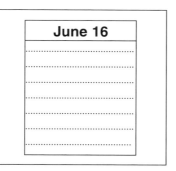   

| June 11 | June 16 | June 30 |

A, ☐   B ☐   C ☐

PART 2

QUESTIONS 6–10

Listen to Rose talking to Steve about her day.

What is Rose going to do at each time?

For questions 6–10, write a letter A–H next to each time.

You will hear the conversation twice.

EXAMPLE

0 9.00 a.m. ☐ E

TIMES

6 10.00 a.m. ☐

7 11.00 a.m. ☐

8 12.00 a.m. ☐

9 1.00 p.m. ☐

10 2.00 p.m. ☐

ACTIVITIES

A art lesson

B have lunch

C help Steve

D meet Bill

E see doctor

F see teacher

G study

H swim

PART 3

QUESTIONS 11–15

Listen to Peter talking to a friend about learning to drive.
For questions 11–15, tick ☑ A, B or C.
You will hear the conversation twice.

EXAMPLE	ANSWER
0 The name of Peter's driving school is	
A AA.	☐
B AC.	☐
C ABC.	☑

11 Each driving lesson costs

A ⌄ £14. ☐

B £40. ☐

C £60. ☐

12 A lesson is

A 30 minutes. ☐

B ⌄ 45 minutes. ☐

C 60 minutes. ☐

13 The teacher's car is

A ⌄ slow. ☐

B old. ☐

C big. ☐

14   Peter failed the test because he

    A   drove too fast. ☐

    B   didn't see a crossing. ☐

    C   didn't stop at the traffic lights. ☐

15   Peter thinks the teacher is too

    A   expensive. ☐

    B   unfriendly. ☐

    C   young. ☐

PART 4

QUESTIONS 16–20

You will hear a man asking about theatre tickets.
Listen and complete questions 16–20.
You will hear the conversation twice.

PLAYHOUSE THEATRE

EVENING SHOW:	The White Room
Time:	**16** 7:30
AFTERNOON SHOW:	**17** The School Bus
Time:	3 o'clock
Ticket prices:	**18** £15 and £ 12.50
All tickets £6 on:	**19** MONDAY
Car park in:	**20** STUART .... Street

PART 5

QUESTIONS 21–25

You will hear some information about a health centre.

Listen and complete questions 21–25.

You will hear the information twice.

MILL HOUSE HEALTH CENTRE

Opens again tomorrow at:		8 a.m.
Phone number (for appointments):	**21**	793290
Phone after:	**22**	8:30am
Get medicines from:	**23**	WADLEYS .... Chemist's Shop
Bus number:	**24**	77 to HEANS;
For accidents, go to:	**25**	UNIVERSIT HOSPITAL .... Hospital

---

You now have 8 minutes to write your answers on the answer sheet.

PAPER 3   SPEAKING (8–10 minutes)

The Speaking test lasts 8 to 10 minutes. You will take the test with another candidate. There are two examiners, but only one of them will talk to you. The examiner will ask you questions and ask you to talk to the other candidate.

Part 1 (5–6 minutes)

The examiner will ask you and your partner some questions. These questions will be about your daily life, past experience and future plans. For example, you may have to speak about your school, job, hobbies or home town.

Part 2 (3–4 minutes)

You and your partner will speak to each other. You will ask and answer questions. The examiner will give you a card with some information on it. The examiner will give your partner a card with some words on it. Your partner will use the words on the card to ask you questions about the information you have. Then you will change roles.

Test 3

PART 1

QUESTIONS 1–5

Which notice (A–H) says this (1–5)?

For questions 1–5, mark the correct letter A–H on the answer sheet.

EXAMPLE	ANSWER
0 We sell clothes.	**F**

1 This is only for young people.

2 Go to the next floor if you want a drink.

3 You cannot drive here today.

4 We are open every day.

5 Do not bring your lunch in here.

A MOTORWAY AHEAD – NO BICYCLES OR LEARNER DRIVERS

B COFFEE MACHINE UPSTAIRS

C DANGER – FOG! MOTORWAY CLOSED

D COMPUTER ROOM No food or drinks inside

E Restaurant closed Tuesday and Thursday lunchtime

F Ladies' and children's coats upstairs

G Kenyan Coffee Centre Opening hours: 8 a.m. – 6 p.m. daily

H Under 12s swimming course Saturday 10 a.m.

PART 2

QUESTIONS 6–10

Read the sentences (6–10) about a shopping trip.
Choose the best word (A, B or C) for each space.
For questions 6–10, mark A, B or C on the answer sheet.

EXAMPLE	ANSWER
0 Jack .... to buy a new pair of shoes for school.	**C**
A enjoyed **B** got **C** needed	

6   He .... a bus to the big department store in the centre of town.

  A   travelled   **B**   went   **C**   took

7   The shoes were on the top .... near to the café.

  A   stairs   **B**   floor   **C**   room

8   The assistant showed Jack several pairs but they were all the .... size.

  A   wrong   **B**   different   **C**   big

9   Then he .... on some red and black leather football boots.

  A   tried   **B**   wore   **C**   chose

10   'They're not too .... so I'll have them,' Jack said.

  A   high   **B**   great   **C**   expensive

PART 3

QUESTIONS 11–15

Complete the five conversations.

For conversations 11–15, mark A, B or C on the answer sheet.

EXAMPLE		ANSWER
How old are you?	A I'm 18. B I'm Sally. C I'm fine.	A

11   It's my sister's birthday tomorrow!

    A, Happy New Year!

    B, Is she going to have a party?

    C, How old are they?

12   Mary will help the teacher.

    A, Are you certain?

    B, Do you understand?

    C, Can you hear?

13   I would like to see the doctor.

    A, I hope you'll feel better soon.

    B, It hurts a lot.

    C, Have you got an appointment?

14   Shall we leave now?

    A, Have you got time?

    B, Near the station?

    C, I'd like to stay.

15   Anything else?

    A, No, it isn't.

    B, Not at all.

    C, Not today, thanks.

QUESTIONS 16–20

Complete the conversation.

What does Chris say to the waiter?

For questions 16–20, mark the correct letter A–H on the answer sheet.

EXAMPLE		ANSWER
Waiter:	Good evening. Can I help you?	
Chris:	0	G

Waiter:	I'm afraid we haven't got a table free at the moment.	**A**	I'd like a salad and a main course.
Chris:	16	**B**	How long will we have to wait?
Waiter:	About a quarter of an hour. Those people in the corner have nearly finished.	**C**	Yes, we'll have two glasses of mineral water.
Chris:	17	**D**	Right. Where can we leave our coats?
Waiter:	Of course. Can I bring you a drink?	**E**	I need to make a telephone call.
Chris:	18		
Waiter:	Certainly. Anything else I can do for you?	**F**	We'll go somewhere else.
Chris:	19	**G**	Have you got a table for two, please?
Waiter:	There's a phone outside the kitchen.	**H**	That's all right. Can we see the menu, please?
Chris:	20		
Waiter:	I'll take them for you. Your table will be ready soon.		

PART 4

QUESTIONS 21–27

Read the article about some pop stars.

Are sentences 21–27 'Right' (A) or 'Wrong' (B)?

If there is not enough information to answer 'Right' (A) or 'Wrong' (B), choose 'Doesn't say' (C).

For questions 21–27, mark A, B or C on the answer sheet.

HOW DO THE IRISH POP-GROUP 'BOYZONE' LIVE A HEALTHY LIFE?

Stephen:	Sleeping well is very important. When I can get home to my mother's house, I sleep for ten hours. But I find it very difficult to sleep at night after a concert because my head is full of music.
Keith:	Sport is important. Before I had a car accident I was at the sports centre two and a half hours a day, five days a week. I can't do that now so I do about 150 sit-ups a day.
Ronan:	I don't drink alcohol or smoke. I try to eat well. Also I drink a lot of water because it's good for your health. I should have about eight glasses a day but I don't always drink so much.
Shane:	People shouldn't work all the time. I love my job but there are other things I like doing too. In my free time I just listen to music or watch TV. It's good for you to do nothing sometimes.
Mikey:	I don't get tired any more since the doctor told me to eat better. Now I eat lots of things like carrots and spinach every day. But I still eat burgers sometimes!

EXAMPLE	ANSWER
0 Stephen sleeps well in his mother's house. **A** Right **B** Wrong **C** Doesn't say	**A**

21   Stephen thinks a lot about music after a concert.

A,   Right   **B,**   Wrong   **C,**   Doesn't say

22   Keith's accident happened last year.

A,   Right   **B,**   Wrong   **C,**   Doesn't say

23   Keith goes to the sports centre five days a week now.

A ,   Right   **B,**   Wrong   **C,**   Doesn't say

24   Ronan thinks he drinks enough water every day.

A,   Right   **B,**   Wrong   **C,**   Doesn't say

25   Shane is only happy when he's working.

A,   Right   **B,**   Wrong   **C,**   Doesn't say

26   Mikey was often tired before he started eating vegetables.

A,   Right   **B ,**   Wrong   **C,**   Doesn't say

27   Mikey's favourite food is burgers.

A ,   Right   **B,,**   Wrong   **C,**   Doesn't say

PART 5

QUESTIONS 28–35

Read the article about a picture on a hill.

Choose the best word (A, B or C) for each space (28–35).

For questions 28–35, mark A, B or C on the answer sheet.

The Cerne Giant

Sherborne and Dorchester are two towns ......**0**...... the south of England that are quite near each other. On the road between them, ...**28**...... are a lot of green hills and fields. On one of ......**29**...... hills is a picture of a very large man. The man in the picture is called the *Cerne Giant* because the village that is ......**30**...... to him is called Cerne.

    Nobody really ......**31**...... when the *Cerne Giant* was made, but people think that it was a very ......**32**...... time ago. To ......**33**...... nearer the picture, you can walk from Cerne. If you ......**34**...... on the first of May when the sun comes up, you will see all the people ......**35**...... the village dancing around the man on the hill.

EXAMPLE			ANSWER
0 **A** in	**B** on	**C** at	**A**

28	**A** there	**B** they	**C** where
29	**A** another	**B** its	**C** these
30	**A** beside	**B** next	**C** behind
31	**A** known	**B** knows	**C** know
32	**A** longest	**B** long	**C** longer
33	**A** get	**B** got	**C** getting
34	**A** go	**B** goes	**C** going
35	**A** on	**B** at	**C** from

PART 6

QUESTIONS 36–40

Read the descriptions (36–40) of some things you may find at a party.

What is the word for each description?

The first letter is already there. There is one space for each other letter in the word.

For questions 36–40, write the words on the answer sheet.

EXAMPLE	ANSWER
0 Everybody likes to eat a piece of this.	c _a_ _k_ _e_

36 You need this if you want to dance.

m _ _ _ _

37 If it's your birthday, your guests may give you this.

p _ _ _ _ _ _

38 You need this to put your drink in.

g _ _ _ _

39 You can buy this drink in a bottle or a can.

l _ _ _ _ _ _ _ _

40 You hope these people will come to your party.

f _ _ _ _ _ _ _

PART 7

QUESTIONS 41–50

Complete the letter.

Write ONE word for each space (41–50).

For questions 41–50, write your words on the answer sheet.

Dear Lorna,

How (**Example:** .....*are*.....) you? I'm happy because .... **41** ....
month I got a new job in the city centre. I .... **42** ....
working in a Tourist Information Office and .... **43** .... is
very interesting. I start work .... **44** .... morning at half
past seven, so I .... **45** .... to get up very early! I love
this job because I meet people from a .... **46** .... of
different countries. I like telling them .... **47** .... our
city. Here is .... **48** α photo of me. I'm .... **49** .... my new
uniform. .... **50** .... you like it?

Love,

Gloria

PART 8

QUESTIONS 51–55

Read the two e-mail messages.

Fill in the Flower Order Form.

For questions 51–55, write the information on the answer sheet.

To:	Stephen Jones
Date:	21 August

Stephen!
Remember it's your sister's birthday tomorrow. She'll be 16. Have you got her new address in York? She lives in Shirley Road now, at number 47.

Mother

To:	Mary Jones
Date:	21 August

Don't worry Mum! I won't forget Lulu's special day tomorrow! I'm getting her some flowers – Garden Gate Flowers will send them for £15 or £20. I'll choose the cheaper ones, of course, with a nice card saying 'Happy Birthday'!

Stephen

Garden Gate Flowers
Flower Order Form

From: *Stephen Jones*

To: **51**

Date: **52**

Address: **53**

Price: **54**

Message on card: **55**

PART 9

QUESTION 56

You want to sell your bicycle and you see this notice at your college.

<u>BICYCLE WANTED</u>

HAVE YOU GOT A BICYCLE TO SELL?

HOW MUCH IS IT? HOW OLD IS IT?

WHEN CAN I SEE IT?

(Leave a note in reception for Gary Jones.)

Write a note to Gary Jones. Answer his questions about your bicycle.

Write 25–35 words.

Write your note on the answer sheet.

PAPER 2   LISTENING (approximately 30 minutes including 8 minutes transfer time)

PART 1
QUESTIONS 1–5

You will hear five short conversations.

You will hear each conversation twice.

There is one question for each conversation.

For questions 1–5, put a tick ☑ under the right answer.

EXAMPLE

0   How many people were at the meeting?

3	**13**	**30**
A ☐	B ☐	C ☑

---

1   When will they go on holiday?

June	**July**	**September**
A, ☐	B ☐	C ☐

2   How is Patti going to travel?

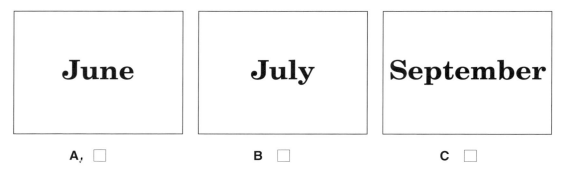

A ☐   B ☐   C, ☐

3   What will Sam do?

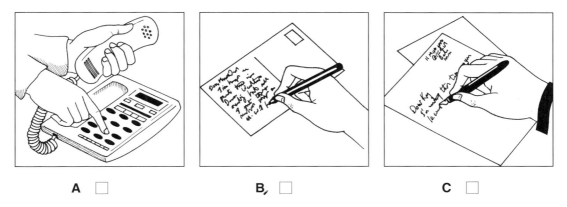

A ☐   **B,** ☐   **C** ☐

4   What was the weather like in Portugal?

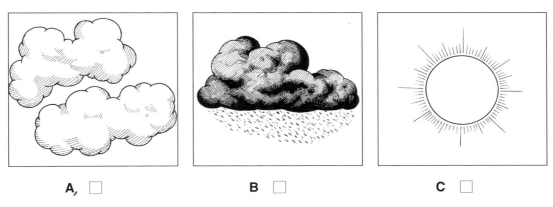

A, ☐   **B** ☐   **C** ☐

5   What has the girl broken?

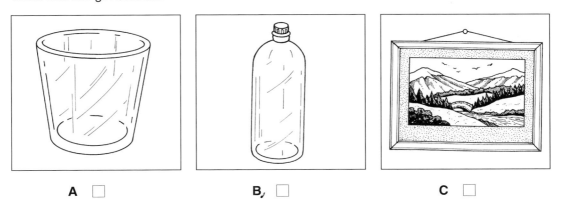

A ☐   **B,** ☐   **C** ☐

PART 2

QUESTIONS 6–10

Listen to Patrick talking to his mother about a photo of his old school friends.
What is each person wearing?
For questions 6–10, write a letter A–H next to each person.
You will hear the conversation twice.

EXAMPLE

0 Peter D

PEOPLE

6 Martin F

7 Joanna A

8 Amy B

9 James C

10 Robert H

THEIR CLOTHES

A coat

B dress

C hat

D jacket

E jeans

F shirt

G sweater

H t-shirt

PART 3

QUESTIONS 11–15

Listen to Jenny asking Mark about school holiday activities.
For questions 11–15, tick ☑ A, B or C.
You will hear the conversation twice.

EXAMPLE	ANSWER
0 The children's show is at	
A the theatre.	☐
B the shopping centre.	☐
C the library.	☑

11   The show begins at

A   1.15. ☐

B   2.00. ☐

C   3.30. ☐

12   A child's ticket costs

A   25p. ☐

B   75p. ☐

C   £1.50. ☐

13   The holiday reading course is for

A   4 weeks. ☐

B   6 weeks. ☐

C   10 weeks. ☐

14   This year from the library, children can win

    A,   a pen. ☐

    B   a school bag. ☐

    C   a book. ☐

15   Jenny should meet Mark again

    A   next week. ☐

    B   tomorrow. ☐

    C,   today. ☐

PART 4

QUESTIONS 16–20

You will hear Judy asking about music lessons.

Listen and complete questions 16–20.

You will hear the conversation twice.

GUITAR LESSONS
FOR JUDY

Class:		Beginners
Day:	**16**	WEDNESDAY
Starting time:	**17**	7:30pm
Price of each lesson:	**18**	£ 5.50
Teacher's name:	**19**	Mrs CAPELLE
Room number:	**20**	328

PART 5

QUESTIONS 21–25

You will hear a teacher talking about a school trip.

Listen and complete questions 21–25.

You will hear the information twice.

SCHOOL TRIP

Day: Saturday

Visit: **21** FILM MUSEM

Leave at: **22** 8.45

Meet in: **23** CAR PARK

Cost: **24** £ 6.70 each

Bring: **25** PENCIL

You now have 8 minutes to write your answers on the answer sheet.

PAPER 3   SPEAKING (8–10 minutes)

The Speaking test lasts 8 to 10 minutes. You will take the test with another candidate. There are two examiners, but only one of them will talk to you. The examiner will ask you questions and ask you to talk to the other candidate.

Part 1 (5–6 minutes)

The examiner will ask you and your partner some questions. These questions will be about your daily life, past experience and future plans. For example, you may have to speak about your school, job, hobbies or home town.

Part 2 (3–4 minutes)

You and your partner will speak to each other. You will ask and answer questions. The examiner will give you a card with some information on it. The examiner will give your partner a card with some words on it. Your partner will use the words on the card to ask you questions about the information you have. Then you will change roles.

Test 4

PAPER 1   READING AND WRITING (1 hour 10 minutes)

PART 1
QUESTIONS 1–5

Which notice (A–H) says this (1–5)?
For questions 1–5, mark the correct letter A–H on the answer sheet.

EXAMPLE	ANSWER
0 You can only get small pictures here.	**H**

1   You can use this for two days.

2   Students do not have to pay to go here at weekends.

3   Someone would like to speak another language.

4   If you study here, you will pay less for this.

5   You can find things to listen to here in the college.

A
> **WANTED**
> Spanish lessons
> evenings or weekends

B
> **English Language Student Library**
> **books, magazines and cassettes**

C
> College Film Night
> 'TITANIC'
> College students £2.50   Others £3.00

D
> **The Biggest Video Store in Town**
> **OPEN 24 HOURS**

E
> **YORK MUSEUM**
> Mon–Fri   **£5**
> Sat–Sun   **£2 / Students free**

F
> **Weekend Travel Card £10**
> **Train or Bus**
> **Central London only**

G
> Learn to play the guitar in four months
> Video course – £50

H
> Colour Photos
> Passport size only 4 for £3

PART 2

QUESTIONS 6–10

Read the sentences (6–10) about Jane's hobby.
Choose the best word (A, B or C) for each space.
For questions 6–10, mark A, B or C on the answer sheet.

EXAMPLE	ANSWER
0 Jane's .... hobby is taking photographs.	B
A happy **B** favourite **C** excellent	

6   She hopes to .... a photographer for a newspaper one day.

   A   work   **B,** become   **C**   do

7   She .... a photography club to learn more about using a camera.

   A   made   **B**   went   **C,** joined

8   Jane says it's .... to take pictures of children or animals because they are always moving.

   A   careful   **B,** hard   **C**   fast

9   There was a .... about a competition in a photography magazine.

   A, notice   **B**   bill   **C**   ticket

10   Jane .... the first prize for one of her pictures.

   A, won   **B**   carried   **C**   caught

PART 3

QUESTIONS 11–15

Complete the five conversations.

For conversations 11–15, mark A, B or C on the answer sheet.

EXAMPLE

Where do you come from?

A   New York.
B   School.
C   Home.

ANSWER

A

11   When will lunch be ready?

A, Quite soon.
B   It's soup and toast.
C   I hope you're hungry.

12   It's very hot in here.

A   Do you feel cold?
B   I'll turn on the heating.
C, Let's go outside then.

13   Have you met Henry before?

A   Yes, at first.
B, Yes, on holiday.
C   Yes, I do.

14   Do you like visiting museums?

A   I'd love to!
B   No, I haven't.
C, Not really.

15   I've broken my glasses.

A, Here's another one.
B   You can't see.
C, That's a pity!

QUESTIONS 16–20

Complete the conversation.

What does the student say to the assistant in the tourist information office?

For questions 16–20, mark the correct letter A–H on the answer sheet.

EXAMPLE		ANSWER
Assistant:	Hello, can I help you?	
Student:	0	H

Assistant:	Do you want the university tennis courts or the city ones?	A	Thank you. I'll go there now.
		B	I suppose so.
Student:	16 .... *C*		
		C	Oh, are there different ones? I didn't know.
Assistant:	Yes. Are you a university student? They can use the university ones.		
		D	That's fine. Is Park Street just after the High Street?
Student:	17 .... *G*		
Assistant:	So, you need the city tennis courts. They're in Park Street.	E	Can I use them?
		F	Is that far from here?
Student:	18 .... *F*		
Assistant:	Well, if you walk, it's about 20 minutes.	G	Well, I'm a student at a language school, not the university.
Student:	19 .... *D*		
Assistant:	That's right. Take the third road on the left, then it's on the right.	H	Yes, please. Where are the tennis courts?
Student:	20 .... *A*		
Assistant:	You're welcome.		

PART 4

QUESTIONS 21–27

Read the article about a singer.

Are sentences 21–27 'Right' (A) or 'Wrong' (B)?

If there is not enough information to answer 'Right' (A) or 'Wrong' (B), choose 'Doesn't say' (C).

For questions 21–27, mark A, B or C on the answer sheet.

John Pickering

In a park in a small town in central England, John Pickering cuts the grass and waters the flowers. But all last week he was in Tokyo and millions of Japanese people watched the thirty-five-year-old gardener on television because John is the number one singer in Japan at the moment. John visited Japan a few months ago to sing in dance clubs in Osaka and Nagoya. A disc jockey heard his songs and played them on his radio show. Hundreds of young people phoned the radio and asked the disc jockey to play the songs once more.

John, who uses the name Jon Otis when he sings in Japan, is not going to stop working in the park in England. He does not know yet how much he will earn from his music. 'I must keep my job in the park,' he says. 'I still have to pay my bills!' The other gardeners do not know that he is famous in Japan. They've never even heard him sing.

John's wife, Denise, a hospital worker, says, 'This will not change the way we live. I only know John Pickering, not Jon Otis!'

EXAMPLE	ANSWER
0 John Pickering usually works in England.	**A**
A Right **B** Wrong **C** Doesn't say	

21   A few days ago, John was on television in Japan.

A, Right   **B** Wrong   **C** Doesn't say

22   John's first show in Japan was on the radio.

A Right   **B,** Wrong   **C** Doesn't say

23   John hopes to become famous in England one day.

A Right   **B,** Wrong   **C,** Doesn't say

24   John Pickering and Jon Otis are the same person.

A, Right   **B** Wrong   **C** Doesn't say

25   John will still work in the park because he needs the money.

A, Right   **B** Wrong   **C** Doesn't say

26   John's colleagues think his songs are very good.

A Right   **B,** Wrong   **C** Doesn't say

27   John's wife would like him to stop singing.

A Right   **B** Wrong   **C,** Doesn't say

PART 5

QUESTIONS 28–35

Read the article about postcards.

Choose the best word (A, B or C) for each space (28–35).

For questions 28–35, mark A, B or C on the answer sheet.

POSTCARDS

Today, people like to send postcards ......**0**...... their
friends and family. These postcards often ......**28**......
pictures of beaches, mountains or castles on them and
you ......**29**...... write a message on the back. Many people send postcards ......**30**...... they
are on holiday because postcards are cheap and the pictures on them are often
......**31**...... than people's own photos.

Somebody sent the first postcard ......**32**...... the end of the nineteenth century. It had a
picture of a town by the sea on it. Later on, postcards had pictures showing
something in the news that week, perhaps an accident ......**33**...... an important person's
visit. People liked to ......**34**...... them because they did ......**35**...... have pictures in their
newspapers then.

EXAMPLE			ANSWER
0 **A** to	**B** by	**C** from	**A**

28   **A**   had   **B**   has   **C**   have

29   **A**   can   **B**   shall   **C**   do

30   **A**   until   **B**   when   **C**   during

31   **A**   best   **B**   better   **C**   good

32   **A**   at   **B**   in   **C**   on

33   **A**   also   **B**   too   **C**   or

34   **A**   see   **B**   saw   **C**   seen

35   **A**   never   **B**   not   **C**   no

PART 6

QUESTIONS 36–40

Read the descriptions (36–40) of some things you may learn about in a geography lesson.

What is the word for each description?

The first letter is already there. There is one space for each other letter in the word.

For questions 36–40, write the words on the answer sheet.

EXAMPLE	ANSWER
0 This is a large group of trees.	f _o_ _r_ _e_ _s_ _t_

36 You may find snow on the top of this at all times of the year.

m _o_ _u_ _n_ _t_ _a_ _i_ _n_

37 The farmer puts animals or plants here.

f _i_ _e_ _l_ _d_

38 People have to cross water to get to this.

i _s_ _l_ _a_ _n_ _d_

39 The water in this starts in the hills and runs to the sea.

r _i_ _v_ _e_ _r_

40 Engineers build this to take things in boats from one place to another.

c _a_ _n_ _a_ _l_

PART 7

QUESTIONS 41–50

Complete the letter.
Write ONE word for each space (41–50).
For questions 41–50, write your words on the answer sheet.

Dear Mrs Brian,

I (**Example:** ......*am*......) sorry but I can't come to your class
....**41**.... more because I have ....**42**.... return to my country.
My sister is going to get married ....**43**.... month. I want
to go shopping ....**44**.... her to choose a dress. My parents
....**45**.... going to make a big meal for the guests and there
will ....**46**.... a lot of work in the kitchen.

I'm sorry I ....**47**.... leave the English class. You are
....**48**.... very good teacher. Please ....**49**.... goodbye to the
other students for ....**50**....

Thanks again.

Best wishes,

Soraya

75

PART 8

QUESTIONS 51–55

Read the note and the information about music lessons.

Fill in the information on the application form.

For questions 51–55, write the information on the answer sheet.

Dear Mrs Bell,

I would like to join your piano class. I can play some classical music, but now I'd like to learn to play modern music. I have English classes with Mr Smith every morning, but I am free in the afternoons.

Maria Gomez

MUSIC LESSONS

Mrs Bell

Wednesday	10 am	Piano
	2 pm	Guitar
Thursday	9.30 am	Guitar
	3.30 pm	Piano

College Music Lessons
Application Form

Name: *Maria Gomez*

Teacher:	51	Mrs Bell
Musical instrument:	52	PIANO
What kind of music do you want to learn?	53	Modren Music
Day of class:	54	WEDNESDAY THURSDAY
Time of class:	55	10 am 3.30pm

PART 9

QUESTION 56

You are going to go walking with your English friend next Friday. Write a note to your friend.

Say:

- **where** you can go walking
- **what** you are going to wear
- **what** your friend should bring.

Write 25–35 words.

Write your note on the answer sheet.

PAPER 2   LISTENING (approximately 30 minutes including 8 minutes transfer time)

PART 1

QUESTIONS 1–5

You will hear five short conversations.

You will hear each conversation twice.

There is one question for each conversation.

For questions 1–5, put a tick ☑ under the right answer.

EXAMPLE

0   How many people were at the meeting?

3	**13**	**30**
A ☐	B ☐	C ☑

---

1   Which is Tom's mother?

A, ☐   B ☐   C ☐

2   Where will the beach party be?

A ☐   B ☐   C, ☐

3   What will Fiona wear to the dance?

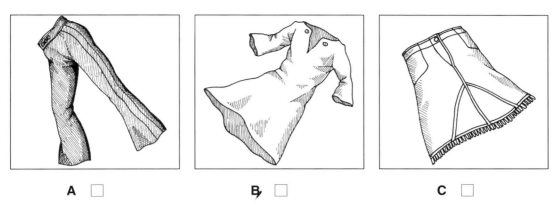

A   ☐   B   ☐   C   ☐

4   What homework is the girl doing now?

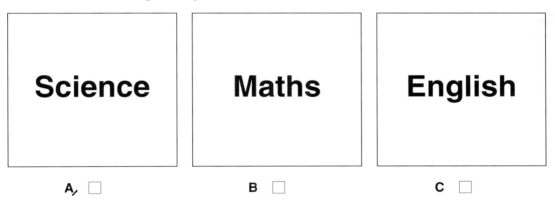

A   ☐   B   ☐   C   ☐

5   What's David going to buy?

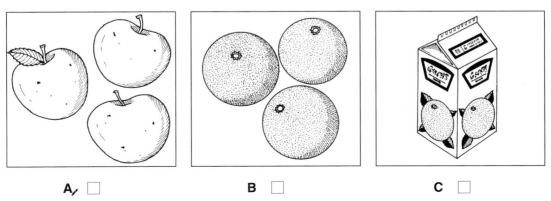

A   ☐   B   ☐   C   ☐

PART 2

QUESTIONS 6–10

Listen to Sonya talking to Martin about her family.

How old are her brothers and sisters?

For questions 6–10, write a letter A–H next to each person.

You will hear the conversation twice.

EXAMPLE

0 Sonya   H

PEOPLE			AGES	
6	Sally	☐	**A**	two
7	Vivienne	☐	**B**	five
			C	seven
8	Roger	☐	**D**	ten
9	Frank	☐	**E**	thirteen
10	Deborah	☐	**F**	fifteen
			G	eighteen
			H	twenty

PART 3

QUESTIONS 11–15

Listen to a woman asking a travel agent for some information about a park in the mountains.

For questions 11–15, tick ✓ A, B or C.

You will hear the conversation twice.

EXAMPLE	ANSWER
0 The woman will visit the park for	
A one week.	✓
B two weeks.	☐
C four weeks.	☐

11   In the park, there is

A   a café.   ☐

B   a hotel.   ☐

C   a guest-house.   ☐

12   The village has a

A   swimming pool.   ☐

B   cinema.   ☐

C   food shop.   ☐

13   You can only go through the park

A   by car.   ☐

B   by bus.   ☐

C   on foot.   ☐

14   On weekdays, a visit to the park costs

    A $12.   ☐

    B $13.   ☐

    C $16.   ☐

15   In the park, the woman will see

    A   animals.   ☐

    B   flowers.   ☐

    C   snow.   ☐

PART 4

QUESTIONS 16–20

You will hear Mats talking to his friend, Sarah, about a trip to Manchester in England.
Listen and complete questions 16–20.
You will hear the conversation twice.

TRIP TO MANCHESTER

Go to Manchester in: *October*

Temperature in autumn: **16** 14 .... *degrees*

Will need to wear: **17** RAIN COAT

Name of train station in London: **18** EUSTON

Cost of train: **19** £ 30

Take Sarah some: **20** CHEESE

PART 5

QUESTIONS 21–25

You will hear some information about a museum.
Listen and complete questions 21–25.
You will hear the information twice.

THE REDFERN MUSEUM

Open: Monday to Thursday

You can see:

    Downstairs   **21** old _CLOTHS_

    Upstairs: pictures by   **22** _PAIN SOANISH_ artists

Concerts during month of: **23** _Nov DEC_

Student ticket: **24** £3.80

Telephone number: **25** 557642

You now have 8 minutes to write your answers on the answer sheet.

PAPER 3 SPEAKING (8–10 minutes)

The Speaking test lasts 8 to 10 minutes. You will take the test with another candidate. There are two examiners, but only one of them will talk to you. The examiner will ask you questions and ask you to talk to the other candidate.

Part 1 (5–6 minutes)

The examiner will ask you and your partner some questions. These questions will be about your daily life, past experience and future plans. For example, you may have to speak about your school, job, hobbies or home town.

Part 2 (3–4 minutes)

You and your partner will speak to each other. You will ask and answer questions. The examiner will give you a card with some information on it. The examiner will give your partner a card with some words on it. Your partner will use the words on the card to ask you questions about the information you have. Then you will change roles.

1A

The White House

Disco

Rock music from the U.S.A.

<u>Over 18s only</u>

Doors open: 9 pm
Tuesday – Saturday

Tickets: £6 (Students £5)
No jeans or T-shirts

2B

<u>ART SHOW</u>

◆ **where?**

◆ **when?**

◆ **whose pictures?**

◆ **ticket? £**

◆ **buy / picture?**

3A

Parker's Sweet Shop

14 Barrett Road
5 minutes from town centre

TRY OUR FAMOUS CHOCOLATE EGGS AND SUGAR HEARTS

Prices lower than in other shops
OPEN MONDAY–SATURDAY 9AM–5PM

4B

A WALK FOR TOURISTS

◆ **where / start?**

◆ **what / visit?**

◆ **every day?**

◆ **expensive?**

◆ **lunch?**

DISCO

◆ **every evening?**

◆ **what music?**

◆ **clothes / wear?**

◆ **student ticket? £?**

◆ **begin?**

ART SHOW

Pictures by David Piper
Meet the artist and buy a painting for your home

6–8pm every evening

Adults: *£4*
Students: *£2*

28 Market Street

3B

SWEET SHOP

◆ **name?**

◆ **expensive?**

◆ **when / open?**

◆ **chocolate eggs?**

◆ **near town centre?**

4A

WALK THROUGH OUR BEAUTIFUL TOWN
FRIENDLY TOUR GUIDES

See the museum, market and castle

Every Tuesday
Starts: Grand Hotel at 10 am
Finishes with lunch in Park Restaurant

£13 per person

1C

PAINTING COMPETITION

For young people 8–16 years old

Paint a picture of an animal

Send it to:
Young Artist Magazine
12 High Street

before 14 September

and win a bicycle!

2D

FILM CLUB

◆ **every week?**

◆ **price? £**

◆ **where / ticket?**

◆ **French films?**

◆ **café?**

3C

GLORIA'S SANDWICH SHOP

We make 100 different sandwiches!

*Hot soup
Orange juice
Coffee*

£2.80 each sandwich

Car park behind shop

Closed on Mondays

4D

CLUB FOR YOUNG PEOPLE

◆ **name?**

◆ **when?**

◆ **what / do?**

◆ **where?**

◆ **cost? £?**

PAINTING COMPETITION

◆ **win something?**

◆ **what / paint?**

◆ **for everybody?**

◆ **competition address?**

◆ **last day?**

2C

CITY UNIVERSITY FILM CLUB

EVERY MONDAY 6–9.30 p.m.

Films from America, Australia and Britain

Get your tickets from the Student Office

Adults	£3
Students	£1.50

Café open for drinks and snacks

3D

SANDWICH SHOP

◆ **what sandwiches?**

◆ **price?**

◆ **open every day?**

◆ **drinks?**

◆ **car park?**

4C

HAPPY DAYS CLUB

for young people from
12–18 years

Every Friday
7.30–10.30 pm

29 Milton Street

Just £2 per week

Games – music – dancing and lots more

Test 1 Key

Paper 1   Reading and Writing

Part 1

1 A   **2** C   **3** D   **4** B   **5** F

Part 2

6 B   **7** A   **8** B   **9** A   **10** C

Part 3

11 A   **12** A   **13** A   **14** B   **15** C
16 H   **17** F   **18** A   **19** D   **20** B

Part 4

21 A   **22** A   **23** A   **24** B   **25** C   **26** C   **27** B

Part 5

28 C   **29** B   **30** C   **31** A   **32** B   **33** C   **34** C   **35** B

Part 6

For questions 36–40, spelling must be correct.

36 key   **37** glasses   **38** money   **39** comb   **40** diary

Part 7

For questions 41–50, ignore capitals / absence of capitals. Spelling must be correct.

41 for   **42** your   **43** was   **44** are   **45** of   **46** they
47 them   **48** am/'m   **49** will/shall/'ll   **50** time/while

Part 8

For questions 51–55, spelling must be correct.

51 Brazilian   **52** (hotel) receptionist   **53** 26 Park Road, Oxford
54 to study English   **55** two/2 months

Part 9

Question 56

The three pieces of information that must be communicated are:

i   how they will get there
ii what time they will arrive
iii what they will do.

Sample answer A

Mark: 5
This is a very good answer with no errors.

> *Dear Paul,*
> *I'm going to visit you on Saturday.*
> *I will come with my car. I will arrive on Saturday morning. First I want*
> *to see you, then we're going to the cinema. After that we're going to*
> *the football match.*
> *See you on Saturday*
> *Yours,*
> *Diego*

Sample answer B

Mark: 4
There are frequent errors in spelling and grammar but they do not require interpretation.

> *Hallo Paul,*
> *I going to visit you on Satyrday. I want stay one week in your haus. I*
> *thing I coming at 6 p.m. whit my car.*
> *I joust want see you and speaking whit you for my problem.*
> *Thank you.*
> *See you!*   *From: Newman*

Sample answer C

Mark: 3
Only two of the three parts of the message are communicated. There is no suggestion about what they should do during their visit.

> *Dear Paul:*
> *I will get here with taxi. I arrive at two o'clock p.m. Please, when I*
> *arrive, can you give me a glass of water? (because I will arrive*
> *thirsty!)*
> *Thanks*
> *Lots of love: Ming*

Sample answer D

Mark: 3
All three parts of the message are attempted, but the errors in the grammar and vocabulary require some interpretation by the reader.

> POSTCARD
> *I and my sister at Saturday morning about to go by bike go to you*
> *home visit you. I want look you new car and you wife.*
> > *OK!*
> > *See you Saturday*
> > *Rod*

Sample answer E

Mark: 1

Although the candidate has written a great deal, only one part of the message, how they will get there, has been communicated.

> *Dear Paul:*
> *I'm very happy, because, I going to visit you on Saturday. Will I get*
> *up maybe at 10:00 o'clock, I drinking my tea and eating my breads*
> *with ham, after I going to your home, in car. Paul was told about*
> *your town or city what's the name's is AntaPagasta. Will my friend*
> *see you in Antofagasta.*
>
> > *Love Valerie*

Paper 2 Listening

Part 1

1 C   **2** A   **3** B   **4** B   **5** A

Part 2

6 A   **7** B   **8** H   **9** D   **10** E

Part 3

11 B   **12** B   **13** A   **14** A   **15** C

Part 4

For questions 16–20, question 16 must be spelt correctly; recognisable spelling is permitted in questions 17–20.

16 Graham/graham   **17** back / back (ache)   **18** 58 (to) 73
19 Tuesday/tuesday   **20** 2.15 / two fifteen, (a) quarter past two/2

Part 5

For questions 21–25, ignore capitals / absence of capitals. Spelling must be correct.

21 2nd   **22** 37 (.00) (each)   **23** 283 0065   **24** South   **25** Trinity

Transcript

This is the Key English Test. Paper 2. Listening. Test number one. There are five parts to the test. Parts One, Two, Three, Four and Five. We will now stop for a moment before we start the test. Please ask any questions now because you mustn't speak during the test.

[pause]

PART 1   *Look at the instructions for Part One.*

[pause]

You will hear five short conversations. You will hear each conversation twice. There is one question for each conversation. For questions 1 to 5, put a tick under the right answer.

Here is an example:
How many people were at the meeting?

Woman:	Were there many people at the meeting?
Man:	About thirty.
Woman:	That's not many.
Man:	No, but more than last time.

[pause]

The answer is 30, so there is a tick in box C.
Now we are ready to start. Look at question one.

[pause]

Question 1   *One. When did Gary start his new job?*

Woman:	Hello, Gary. I haven't seen you since March.
Man:	Hi, Jane. No, I've been busy with my new job.
Woman:	Really? When did you start that?
Man:	May. I left my last job in April.

[pause]

Now listen again.

[repeat]

[pause]

Question 2   *Two. What time does the film start?*

Woman:	Hello, Odeon Cinema.
Man:	Could you tell me what time the film starts, please?
Woman:	Certainly. There are two screenings, one at four thirty and the other at seven.
Man:	Thank you very much.

[pause]

Now listen again.

[repeat]

[pause]

Question 3   *Three. What was the weather like on Saturday?*

Man: Did you have good weather at the beach at the weekend?
Woman: Yes, it was sunny all weekend.
Man: Wasn't it windy too?
Woman: Only on Sunday.

[pause]

Now listen again.

[repeat]

[pause]

Question 4   *Four. Which motorway will they take?*

Woman: I've put the luggage in the car. Can we leave now?
Man: OK. We'll go on the M6 motorway.
Woman: Isn't it faster on the M1 and then the M62?
Man: Yes, usually, but there's been an accident on the M1 so I don't want to
            go that way.

[pause]

Now listen again.

[repeat]

[pause]

Question 5   *Five. Which book does Lorna want?*

Man: Have you finished studying yet, Lorna?
Girl: No, not yet. Could you give me that book, please?
Man: Which one? There are three here. This one on the sofa?
Girl: No, the one on the chair next to the sofa, please.

[pause]

Now listen again.

[repeat]

[pause]

This is the end of Part One. Now look at Part Two.

[pause]

PART 2   *Listen to Sue talking to a friend about her new clothes.*
            Why did Sue decide to buy each thing?
            For questions 6 to 10, write a letter, A to H, next to the clothes.
            You will hear the conversation twice.

[pause]

Friend: Hi, Sue. Have you been to the shops?
Sue: Yes. I had some money for my birthday so I decided to buy some
            clothes.
Friend: I love those purple jeans.
Sue: Yes, I bought them because purple is my favourite colour.

I got a new jacket too. My old one is too small, so I bought this lovely big one.

Friend: It's really great – did you buy a dress?

Sue: I got this one because it was only nine pounds!

Friend: That's not expensive!

Sue: Then I got a sweater to wear with my jeans.

Friend: It's lovely and soft.

Sue: That's why I bought it.

Friend: Anything else?

Sue: A coat. The long one I have is too big and heavy, but this one is really light.

Friend: Did you buy a short white t-shirt like mine?

Sue: Well, I bought a *long* white one. I'll wear it more often than a short one.

[pause]

Now listen again.

[repeat]

[pause]

This is the end of Part Two. Now look at Part Three.

[pause]

PART 3   *Listen to Jan talking to Steve about getting a student travel card.*
For questions 11 to 15, tick A, B or C. You will hear the conversation twice.
Look at questions 11 to 15 now. You have 20 seconds.

[pause]

Now listen to the conversation.

Jan: Hi, Steve!

Steve: Hi, Jan. I'm going to go to London on the train. Come with me!

Jan: But it's cheaper by bus.

Steve: I've got a student travel card. You can get cheap train tickets with it.

Jan: That sounds good. How much does it cost?

Steve: A card for six months is sixteen pounds.

Jan: So how do I get one?

Steve: You need some photographs – one for the card and one for the form.

Jan: Oh. There's a photo machine in the post office. It gives you four photos for three pounds.

Steve: So does the one in the library. But I went to a photographer's shop. It was cheaper.

Jan: I don't have to show my passport or my driving licence, do I?

Steve: That's right, Jan, you only need a letter from your college.

Jan: I'll ask my teacher for one.

Steve: And then you take everything to the tourist office, by the travel agent's.

Jan: Great, next time you go to London, I'll come too!

[pause]

Now listen again.

[repeat]

[pause]

This is the end of Part Three. Now look at Part Four.

[pause]

PART 4   *You will hear a man speaking on the telephone.*
Listen and complete questions 16 to 20. You will hear the conversation twice.

[pause]

Woman:	Waterhouse School, can I help you?
Mr Graham:	Hello, can I leave a message for Mr Brown, please?
Woman:	Yes, of course. What's your name?
Mr Graham:	David Graham.
Woman:	Could you spell your surname for me, please?
Mr Graham:	Yes, it's G-R-A-H-A-M.
Woman:	Right, I've got that. What's the message?
Mr Graham:	Well, I can't teach my classes for a few days because my back's bad again.
Woman:	Oh dear! A bad back.
Mr Graham:	Yes. Can you ask Mr Brown to tell the students to read their course book. They should start at page 58 and read to page 73.
Woman:	OK, I've got that. Anything else?
Mr Graham:	Er yes … tell Mr Brown that I've been to the doctor and I can't come back to work until Tuesday.
Woman:	That's in the morning, is it?
Mr Graham:	No, not until the afternoon. I'll be there for my first class. It starts at quarter past two.
Woman:	Right. I'll tell him. I hope you feel better soon.
Mr Graham:	Thanks very much. Bye.
Woman:	Goodbye.

[pause]

Now listen again.

[repeat]

[pause]

This is the end of Part Four. Now look at Part Five.

[pause]

PART 5   *You will hear some information about a pop concert.*
Listen and complete questions 21 to 25. You will hear the information twice.

[pause]

Man:	You are listening to Radio South. Here is some information about a pop concert. The group Red River will come to London soon. They will be in London from the twenty-eighth of October to the second of November. After that they will be in Oxford from the fourth of November until the ninth. Tickets are quite expensive – they cost thirty-seven pounds each, but half of that money will go to a

children's hospital. Tickets will sell quickly for this famous band so book early. To book a ticket for a London concert, telephone two–eight–three, double 0–six–five between ten a.m. and ten p.m. Have a credit card number ready. The London concerts will be in South Bank Hall. It's very easy to find. The best way to get there is to take the train. The concert hall is in Trinity Street. That's T-R-I-N-I-T-Y Street. See you there.

For classical music lovers …

[pause]

Now listen again.

[repeat]

[pause]

This is the end of Part Five.

You now have eight minutes to write your answers on the answer sheet.

Note: Teacher, stop the recording here and time eight minutes. Remind students when there is **one** minute remaining.

[pause]

This is the end of the test.

Test 2 Key

Paper 1   Reading and Writing

Part 1

1 C   **2** G   **3** A   **4** B   **5** F

Part 2

6 A   **7** C   **8** C   **9** A   **10** B

Part 3

11 C   **12** B   **13** A   **14** B   **15** A
16 C   **17** F   **18** A   **19** E   **20** D

Part 4

21 A   **22** B   **23** A   **24** B   **25** B   **26** C   **27** B

Part 5

28 B   **29** C   **30** B   **31** A   **32** C   **33** C   **34** A   **35** B

Part 6

For questions 36–40, spelling must be correct.
36 garage   **37** bridge   **38** policeman   **39** crossroads   **40** lights

Part 7

For questions 41–50, ignore capitals / absence of capitals. Spelling must be correct.
41 next/this   **42** go/travel/drive   **43** from   **44** It   **45** a/one
46 can   **47** costs/is   **48** at/every   **49** have/need/want   **50** If

Part 8

For questions 51–55, spelling must be correct.
51 Canadian   **52** history   **53** French (and) German   **54** Brown's Hotel
55 August

Part 9

Question 56

The three pieces of information that must be communicated are:

i   why the candidate didn't go to the party last night
ii whether the candidate can meet Chris on Saturday
iii what the candidate wants to do when they meet.

Sample answer A

Mark: 5
All three parts of the message are clearly communicated with only minor spelling errors.

> *Chris I'm sory I could not come on the party last night because I*
> *met my old friends and I went with them to the cinema.*
> *I can meet you on Saterday and we can go to restaurant.*
> > *bye*   *Sophia*

Sample answer B

Mark: 4
All three parts of the message are clearly communicated but there is no open or close so one mark is lost.

> *I am realy sorry for not coming but my mother forbad me to come.*
> *I am free on Saturday, why not go to the cinema.*

Sample answer C

Mark: 3
The second part of the message, whether they can meet Chris on Saturday, has not been communicated.

> *Dear Chris,*
> *I was very ill last night and had to stay in the bed but I'm fine now*
> *and I want to go to the zoo.*
> > *Masaya*

Sample answer D

Mark: 2
The second and third part of the message have been attempted but require interpretation by the reader.

> *Dear Chris.*
> *Excuse me but I'm not possible to go to the party on Saturday.*
> *But you don't have time Oclock. So I'm supposed you telephone me*
> *for the RDV.*
> *My tel in work 01 46 42 33 50. Yes I very happy to meet there are*
> *the restaurand Italien in the streeOl very good, could you like come*
> *at height oclock on Saturday. Big Kiss*   *Anna*

Sample answer E

Mark: 0

The candidate has not completed the task as required and cannot be given a mark.

> *Hello Chris,*
> *My party was very good.*
> *All my friends arrive in at the time. but you couldn't come in and you*
> *didn't ring me up. Whats the matter with you. me and all my friends*
> *missed you, will you ring me again.   Hope to see you soon*
>   *Your Tomas*

Paper 2   Listening

Part 1

1 C   **2** A   **3** A   **4** B   **5** A

Part 2

6 H   **7** F   **8** D   **9** B   **10** A

Part 3

11 A   **12** B   **13** A   **14** C   **15** A

Part 4

For questions 16 to 20, ignore capitals / absence of capitals. Spelling must be correct.
16 7.30 (p.m./pm)/19.30   **17** bus   **18** 12.50   **19** Monday(s)   **20** Stuart

Part 5

For all questions 21 to 25, ignore capitals / absence of capitals. Spelling must be correct, except in question 25, where recognisable spelling is acceptable.
21 793220   **22** (0)8.30 (a.m./am) / half past eight   **23** Padley(')s
24 77   **25** University

Transcript

This is the Key English Test. Paper 2. Listening. Test number two. There are five parts to the test. Parts One, Two, Three, Four and Five. We will now stop for a moment before we start the test. Please ask any questions now because you mustn't speak during the test.

[pause]

PART 1   *Look at the instructions for Part One.*

[pause]

You will hear five short conversations. You will hear each conversation twice. There is one question for each conversation. For questions 1 to 5, put a tick under the right answer.

Here is an example:
How many people were at the meeting?

Woman: Were there many people at the meeting?
Man: About thirty.
Woman: That's not many.
Man: No, but more than last time.

[pause]

The answer is 30, so there is a tick in box C.
Now we are ready to start. Look at question one.

[pause]

Question 1   *One. What colour is Kathy's bedroom now?*

Kathy: Come and look at my bedroom. I've painted it.
Man: What colour this time, Kathy? Green?
Kathy: I decided to paint it blue.
Man: Oh well, that's nicer than before. I hated those pink walls.

[pause]

Now listen again.

[repeat]

[pause]

Question 2   *Two. Which platform does the woman's train leave from?*

Woman: Which is the platform for the train to London?
Man: The fast train leaves from platform six at seven o'clock.
Woman: I want to go to Rugby – does it stop there?
Man: You need the slow train from platform two at seven ten.

[pause]

Now listen again.

[repeat]

[pause]

Question 3   *Three. How is Susan going to get to the airport?*

Man: How are you going to go to the airport on Tuesday, Susan?
Susan: I'm going to take the coach. I can get off just outside the airport.
              A taxi's too expensive.
Man: There's a train you can get. It's very fast.
Susan: That's only at the weekends.

[pause]

Now listen again.

[repeat]

[pause]

Question 4   *Four. Which is Anna's family?*

Man: Tell me about your family, Anna.
Anna: Well, my father's tall with dark hair and my mother's the opposite.
              She's shorter and blonde. Then there's my brother.
Man: Is he older than you?
Anna: He's five years younger.

[pause]

Now listen again.

[repeat]

[pause]

Question 5   *Five. When is Kim's birthday party?*

Man: Are you going to Kim's birthday party? She'll be sixteen in June.
Woman: Oh, yes. It's on the eleventh, isn't it?
Man: That's right. It'll be quite a big party – about thirty people, I think.
Woman: OK. I'll see you there.

[repeat]

[pause]

Now listen again.

[pause]

This is the end of Part One. Now look at Part Two.

[pause]

PART 2   *Listen to Rose talking to Steve about her day.*
          What is Rose going to do at each time?
          For questions 6 to 10, write a letter, A to H, next to each time.
          You will hear the conversation twice.

[pause]
Steve: Hi, Rose. Can you help me with my English homework?
Rose: Er, no, Steve. I'm very busy this morning. At nine o'clock I'm going to
              see the doctor.
Steve: Well, what are you going to do after that?

Rose:	I go swimming every day now – just for one hour – so I'm going to do that at ten.
Steve:	Well, can I meet you at eleven?
Rose:	Sorry, I've got to see my maths teacher then.
Steve:	And then I suppose you'll go to the library to study.
Rose:	Not today! At twelve I must meet Bill. I need to talk to him.
Steve:	So I'll see you at lunchtime. At one o'clock?
Rose:	I'm going to have lunch with Jo then, but you can come too.
Steve:	No, thanks. I'll see you afterwards.
Rose:	Well, I have an art class at two. But I can help you after that.
Steve:	OK. I'll see you at three then.

[pause]

Now listen again.

[repeat]

[pause]

This is the end of Part Two. Now look at Part Three.

[pause]

PART 3 *Listen to Peter talking to a friend about learning to drive.*
For questions 11 to 15, tick A, B or C. You will hear the conversation twice.
Look at questions 11 to 15 now. You have 20 seconds.

[pause]

Now listen to the conversation.

Friend:	Peter, you're learning to drive, aren't you? Do you go to the AA Driving School?
Peter:	Actually it's called the ABC Driving School.
Friend:	Is it expensive? I want to learn to drive.
Peter:	It's cost me a hundred and forty pounds already. I've had ten lessons and each one is fourteen pounds.
Friend:	Is that for an hour?
Peter:	Mm … less than that – about three quarters of an hour.
Friend:	I see. And is the teacher's car new?
Peter:	Yes, and it's not a big car so parking's easy, but it doesn't go very fast!
Friend:	When are you going to take your driving test?
Peter:	I failed it last week. The traffic lights were red but I didn't see them and I couldn't brake in time.
Friend:	Never mind. You can take the test again. Tell me about your teacher. Is he friendly?
Peter:	He's OK, he's quite young and interesting to talk to, but my father will give me my next lessons. He's cheaper!
Friend:	Well, good luck!

[pause]

Now listen again.

[repeat]

[pause]

This is the end of Part Three. Now look at Part Four.

[pause]

PART 4   *You will hear a man asking about theatre tickets.*
Listen and complete questions 16 to 20. You will hear the conversation twice.

[pause]

Woman:	Playhouse Theatre. Can I help you?
Man:	Yes, I'd like some information about the plays that are on next week, please.
Woman:	Certainly. We have two plays next week. *The White Room* is on at seven thirty every evening. Then in the afternoons we have a play by a new young writer. The name of that is *The School Bus*. That's at three o'clock.
Man:	*The School Bus*?
Woman:	Yes, it's a play for children.
Man:	Mmm … and how much are tickets?
Woman:	Well, tickets for seats upstairs cost fifteen pounds and those for downstairs are twelve pounds fifty.
Man:	Are the prices the same for all performances?
Woman:	No, all tickets are six pounds on Mondays. But you'll have to buy them soon if you want some of those.
Man:	OK. And one more thing … is there a car park near the theatre?
Woman:	Yes, in Stuart Street.
Man:	Can you spell that, please?
Woman:	Certainly. It's S-T-U-A-R-T. It's just behind the theatre.
Man:	Thank you for your help.
Woman:	OK. Goodbye.

[pause]

Now listen again.

[repeat]

[pause]

This is the end of Part Four. Now look at Part Five.

[pause]

PART 5   *You will hear some information about a health centre.*
Listen and complete questions 21 to 25. You will hear the information twice.

[pause]

Man:	This is the Mill House Health Centre. The Health Centre is closed until eight o'clock tomorrow morning, but here is some important information. To make an appointment with one of the doctors you can phone us tomorrow. The number is seven nine three double two 0. The Health Centre is always very busy early in the morning so please do not phone before eight-thirty.
	If you want to get medicine, Padley's Chemist's Shop, that's P-A-D-L-E-Y-S, is open until ten p.m. every evening this week,

including Sundays. Take the 77 bus to the High Street. The stop is right outside the shop.

If you need to see a doctor now, please go to the accident department at University Hospital. They are open twenty-four hours a day for accidents and emergencies. Thank you for calling the Mill House Health Centre this evening. Our doctors and nurses will be pleased to answer any more of your questions tomorrow.

[pause]

Now listen again.

[repeat]

[pause]

This is the end of Part Five.

[pause]

You now have eight minutes to write your answers on the answer sheet.

Note: Teacher, stop the recording here and time eight minutes. Remind students when there is **one** minute remaining.

[pause]

This is the end of the test.

Test 3 Key

Paper 1   Reading and Writing

Part 1

1 H   **2** B   **3** C   **4** G   **5** D

Part 2

6 C   **7** B   **8** A   **9** A   **10** C

Part 3

11 B   **12** A   **13** C   **14** C   **15** C
16 B   **17** H   **18** C   **19** E   **20** D

Part 4

21 A   **22** C   **23** B   **24** B   **25** B   **26** A   **27** C

Part 5

28 A   **29** C   **30** B   **31** B   **32** B   **33** A   **34** A   **35** C

Part 6

For questions 36 to 40, spelling must be correct.

36 music   **37** present   **38** glass   **39** lemonade   **40** friends

Part 7

For questions 41 to 50, ignore capitals / absence of capitals. Spelling must be correct.

41 last/this   **42** am/'m   **43** it   **44** each/every   **45** have/need
46 lot/number/variety   **47** about   **48** a   **49** wearing/in   **50** Do

Part 8

For questions 51 to 55, spelling must be correct.

51 Lulu Jones   **52** 22 August   **53** 47 Shirley Road, York
54 £15 / fifteen pounds   **55** Happy Birthday

Part 9

Question 56

The three pieces of information that must be communicated are:

i   how much it costs
ii how old it is
iii when Gary can see it.

Sample answer A

Mark: 5
All three parts of the message are clearly communicated.

> Gary Jones
> I want to sell my bicycle. I bought it 3 years ago, but I've never used it. It costs £25. You can see it every afternoon. Call me at home: 3642562
> Lucy

Sample answer B

Mark: 4
All three parts of the message are communicated but the errors in grammar and spelling prevent it from gaining full marks.

> Gary Jones:
> I have bycycle to sell. It has two years old. I sell for for 50 pence. You can see every morning at school.
> Ling

Sample answer C

Mark: 3
The third part of the message has not been clearly communicated. The reader does not know when the bicycle could be seen as no time for the meeting is provided.

> Dear Gary Jones,
> I have a bicycle to sell. If you want, we can meet in front of the café's college. I will arrive with the bicycle then, if you are interesting, and I will say you all the information about it. the price of the cicycle is £150 and I bought it one month ago.
> José

Sample answer D

Mark: 3

> Dear Gary Jones
> I have a new bicicle to sell./ I bought it last year, but I want to sell it now. The price of the bike is 50 and you could see the bike in my house.
> See you,
> Matthew

Sample answer E

Mark: 2

Only the first two points are communicated and they require patience by the reader. The third part of the message is not attempted.

> Dear Gary Jones
> I've got bicycle is a selled bicycle from shop in Poole. It costs
> £70.00. This is one years ago. I think the you can find.
> by Hiroko

Paper 2   Listening

Part 1

1 A   **2** C   **3** B   **4** A   **5** B

Part 2

6 E   **7** G   **8** B   **9** C   **10** H

Part 3

11 B   **12** B   **13** B   **14** A   **15** C

Part 4

For questions 16 to 20, ignore capitals / absence of capitals. Spelling must be correct, except in question 16, where recognisable spelling is acceptable.
16 Wednesday/Wed   **17** 7.30 (p.m./pm) / 19.30 / seven thirty / half past seven
18 (£)5.50   **19** Capelle   **20** 328 (on 3rd floor)

Part 5

For questions 21 to 25, ignore capitals / absence of capitals. Spelling must be correct, except in question 21, where recognisable spelling is acceptable.
21 film museum(s)   **22** 8.45 (a.m./am) / quarter to nine   **23** (the) car park
24 (£)6.70 (each)   **25** (a) pencil(s)

Transcript

This is the Key English Test. Paper 2. Listening. Test number three. There are five parts to the test. Parts One, Two, Three, Four and Five. We will now stop for a moment before we start the test. Please ask any questions now because you mustn't speak during the test.

[pause]

PART 1   *Look at the instructions for Part One.*

[pause]

You will hear five short conversations. You will hear each conversation twice. There is one question for each conversation. For questions 1 to 5, put a tick under the right answer.

Here is an example:
How many people were at the meeting?

Woman:	Were there many people at the meeting?
Man:	About thirty.
Woman:	That's not many.
Man:	No, but more than last time.

[pause]

The answer is 30, so there is a tick in box C.
Now we are ready to start. Look at question one.

[pause]

Question 1   *One. When will they go on holiday?*

Man 1:	Do you want to come on holiday with me in the summer?
Man 2:	Sure. I can go in June, July or September.
Man 1:	Well, June will be best for me. July's too hot and I have to work in September.
Man 2:	OK. Where shall we go?

[pause]

Now listen again.

[repeat]

[pause]

Question 2   *Two. How is Patti going to travel?*

Patti:	I'm going to go to Vienna on Saturday.
Man:	How long does it take to fly there, Patti?
Patti:	Oh, I'm going to drive.
Man:	Oh yes, you get ill on planes, don't you?
Patti:	Yes, and trains.

[pause]

Now listen again.

[repeat]

[pause]

113

Question 3   *Three. What will Sam do?*

     Mother: You must phone me while you're on holiday, Sam.
     Sam: Telephoning's too expensive. I'll send you a postcard from the camp-site.
     Mother: But I'll want to know you're alright. Can't you send me a letter?
     Sam: I won't have time for writing letters.

     [pause]

     Now listen again.

     [repeat]

     [pause]

Question 4   *Four. What was the weather like in Portugal?*

     Man: What was the weather like in Portugal, Debbie?
     Debbie: It was cloudy every day, but it didn't rain.
     Man: Really? It was lovely and sunny on our holiday in Spain.
     Debbie: Yes, but we were in the north of Portugal and it's different there.

     [pause]

     Now listen again.

     [repeat]

     [pause]

Question 5   *Five. What has the girl broken?*

     Girl: Be careful, Mum, there are some pieces of glass on the floor.
     Mother: You haven't broken that nice picture, have you?
     Girl: It's alright. The lemonade bottle fell on the floor.
     Mother: Oh well, at least it was empty.

     [pause]

     Now listen again.

     [repeat]

     [pause]

     This is the end of Part One. Now look at Part Two.

     [pause]

PART 2   *Listen to Patrick talking to his mother about a photo of his old school friends.*
     What is each person wearing?
     For questions 6 to 10, write a letter, A to H, next to each person.
     You will hear the conversation twice.

     [pause]

     Mother: How was the party with your old school friends, Patrick?
     Patrick: Great, Mother. We've changed a lot since 1990. Look at this photo.
     Mother: Was Peter there?
     Patrick: Yes, this is him in a sports jacket.
     Mother: Oh, yes. And does Martin still wear a t-shirt and dirty jeans?

Patrick:	Well, he's a businessman now, so he can't be dirty. But he was wearing jeans. Look.
Mother:	Oh, yes. And is this person with the long coat Joanna?
Patrick:	It's like her, isn't it, but Joanna's standing next to Amy and wearing a red sweater.
Mother:	Is that Amy? I can't believe it. She's so thin! That black dress doesn't look very good on her.
Patrick:	She's been ill. That man in the big hat is her husband, James.
Mother:	Oh? Isn't that Robert?
Patrick:	No, see the man in the red t-shirt with the blue trousers? That's Robert.
Mother:	How people change!

[pause]

Now listen again.

[repeat]

[pause]

This is the end of Part Two. Now look at Part Three.

[pause]

PART 3   *Listen to Jenny asking Mark about school holiday activities.*
For questions 11 to 15, tick A, B or C. You will hear the conversation twice.
Look at questions 11 to 15 now. You have twenty seconds.

[pause]

Now listen to the conversation.

Mark:	Hello, Jenny. What are you doing here?
Jenny:	Mark! Hello! This is my daughter, Sarah. It's the school holidays so we're shopping now – we're not sure what to do after that.
Mark:	Well, there's a show for children this afternoon in the library where I work.
Jenny:	Oh? What time is the show?
Mark:	It starts at two and finishes at three thirty. It's only quarter past one now. What about that?
Jenny:	How much is a ticket?
Mark:	Well, it's one pound fifty for adults and seventy-five pence for children. Programmes are twenty-five pence.
Jenny:	And does your library do a reading course in the holidays?
Mark:	Yes, and if children under ten, like Sarah, read four books in six weeks, we give them something to take home.
Jenny:	What, like, a book?
Mark:	Well, this year it's a pen but sometimes it's a book or a school bag. Meet me after the show and I'll tell you what to do.
Jenny:	Thanks. See you later then.

[pause]

Now listen again.

[repeat]

[pause]

This is the end of Part Three. Now look at Part Four.

[pause]

PART 4   *You will hear Judy asking about music lessons.*
Listen and complete questions 16 to 20. You will hear the conversation twice.

[pause]

Man: Good morning. Central School of Music.

Judy: Good morning. My name's Judy Black. I'd like some information about guitar lessons, please.

Man: Are you a beginner?

Judy: Yes, I've never played the guitar before.

Man: Then you'll want a beginners' class. There's one on Wednesday evening and another on Tuesday morning.

Judy: I work during the day so I'd like the evening class.

Man: It begins at half past seven and it's a two-hour class.

Judy: Oh, that will be fine for me. Er, can you tell me how much I have to pay?

Man: Each lesson costs five pounds fifty. That's fifty-five pounds for a course of ten lessons.

Judy: That's not bad. But I haven't got a guitar. Does it matter?

Man: No, the school can lend you one.

Judy: Oh good. And can you tell me the name of the teacher?

Man: It's Mrs Capelle. That's C-A-P-E-L-L-E.

Judy: Right. What room will my lesson be in?

Man: Classroom number three hundred and twenty-eight on the third floor.

Judy: Great. Thank you very much. Bye.

Man: Bye.

[pause]

Now listen again.

[repeat]

[pause]

This is the end of Part Four. Now look at Part Five.

[pause]

PART 5   *You will hear a teacher talking about a school trip.*
Listen and complete questions 21 to 25. You will hear the information twice.

[pause]

Teacher: Right, listen carefully, everyone. I want to tell you about our school trip. We're going to go on Saturday. I hope you can all come. As you know, we're going to visit the film museum. There are lots of very interesting things there about the cinema and how films are made. We'll have to leave at eight forty-five so don't be late. We'll get there by bus. Please meet me in the car park. You all know where that is, don't you? And when we return, the bus will leave you at the school entrance. Tell your parents, won't you?

What next? Oh yes, the cost. It'll be six pounds seventy pence each, OK? Remember to get the money from your parents.

Now, I'm going to give you some work to do at the museum. You'll need to write things down, so take a pencil with you. We'll have lunch in the museum café so you needn't bring any food with you. Well, I think that's everything …

[pause]

Now listen again.

[repeat]

[pause]

This is the end of Part Five.

You now have eight minutes to write your answers on the answer sheet.

Note: Teacher, stop the recording here and time eight minutes. Remind students when there is **one** minute remaining.

[pause]

This is the end of the test.

Test 4 Key

Paper 1   Reading and Writing

Part 1

1 F   **2** E   **3** A   **4** C   **5** B

Part 2

6 B   **7** C   **8** B   **9** A   **10** A

Part 3

11 A   **12** C   **13** B   **14** C   **15** C
16 C   **17** G   **18** F   **19** D   **20** A

Part 4

21 A   **22** B   **23** C   **24** A   **25** A   **26** B   **27** C

Part 5

28 C   **29** A   **30** B   **31** B   **32** A   **33** C   **34** A   **35** B

Part 6

For questions 36 to 40, spelling must be correct.

36 mountain   **37** field   **38** island   **39** river   **40** canal

Part 7

For questions 41 to 50, ignore capitals / absence of capitals. Spelling must be correct.

41 any   **42** to   **43** next/this   **44** with   **45** are   **46** be
47 will/shall/'ll/must   **48** a   **49** say   **50** me

Part 8

For questions 51 to 55, spelling must be correct. Capital letters must be used where indicated.

51 Mrs Bell   **52** piano   **53** modern (music)   **54** Thursday
55 3.30 p.m. / pm

Part 9

Question 56

The three pieces of information that must be communicated are:

i   where you can go walking
ii what you are going to wear
iii what your friend should bring.

Sample answer A

Mark: 5

All three parts of the message are clearly communicated with only occasional grammatical errors.

> *Hi Peter*
> *Let's go walking in my town and go to the park. I will wearing my new skirt bring a camera to the park we will taking some photos.*
> *Love   Nicole*

Sample answer B

Mark: 4

All three parts of the message are communicated but the errors in spelling and grammar prevent it scoring full marks.

> *Hello Jane!*
> *I'm very glade we can go walking next Friday in shopping centre, but I'm not sure the time, I lets to know soon. For me, I wear same dress and you should to bring some money.*
> *See you soon*
> *Andrea*

Sample answer C

Mark: 3

Only two parts of the message are communicated but the candidate does not say what he is going to wear.

> *Hi Jerry, How are you? friday we can walking in country, near by my house.*
> *We going to take food for eat our lunch there so bring it too.*
> *goodbye*
> *Hugo*

Sample answer D

Mark: 3

All three parts of the message are attempted but the first part, where they will walk, requires interpretation.

> *Hi*
> *I can come walking to you on next friday for see you. I going to wear my jeans, t-shirt and tennis. You should bring sunglasses.*
> > *See you Friday*
> > > *Marco*

Sample answer E

Mark: 0

The message is not communicated as required so a mark cannot be given.

> *Shall we go walking next Friday.*
> *Where can you go walking?*
> *What you going to wear?*
> *What should your friend bring?*

Paper 2   Listening

Part 1

1 A   **2** C   **3** B   **4** A   **5** A

Part 2

6 F   **7** E   **8** C   **9** B   **10** G

Part 3

11 A   **12** C   **13** C   **14** A   **15** B

Part 4

For questions 16 to 20, ignore capitals / absence of capitals. Spelling must be correct, except in questions 16, 17 and 20, where recognisable spelling is acceptable.

16 14 degrees   **17** raincoat   **18** Euston   **19** £30 / thirty pounds   **20** cheese

Part 5

For questions 21 to 25, ignore capitals / absence of capitals. Spelling must be correct, except in questions 21, 22 and 23, where recognisable spelling is acceptable.

21 clothes   **22** Spanish   **23** December   **24** (£)3.80   **25** 557642

Transcript

This is the Key English Test. Paper 2. Listening. Test number four. There are five parts to the test. Parts One, Two, Three, Four and Five. We will now stop for a moment before we start the test. Please ask any questions now because you mustn't speak during the test.

[pause]

PART 1   *Look at the instructions for Part One.*

[pause]

You will hear five short conversations. You will hear each conversation twice. There is one question for each conversation. For questions 1 to 5, put a tick under the right answer.

Here is an example:
How many people were at the meeting?

Woman: Were there many people at the meeting?
Man: About thirty.
Woman: That's not many.
Man: No, but more than last time.

[pause]

The answer is 30, so there is a tick in box C.
Now we are ready to start. Look at question one.

[pause]

Question 1   *One. Which is Tom's mother?*

Woman: Is that your mother with the hat, Tom?
Tom: She never wears a hat.
Woman: Has she still got glasses and long hair?
Tom: Her hair's short now. But she still wears glasses.

[pause]

Now listen again.

[repeat]

[pause]

Question 2   *Two. Where will the beach party be?*

Man: Hi, Jane. Going to the beach party tonight?
Jane: Yes. Is it in the same place as last week's – by the boats?
Man: It's going to be by the trees this time.
Jane: I'll meet you at the café then.

[pause]

Now listen again.

[repeat]

[pause]

Question 3   *Three. What will Fiona wear to the dance?*

Fiona: Shall I wear this skirt or my new trousers to the dance tonight, Mum?
Mother: What about your blue dress, Fiona?
Fiona: Is it clean? If it is, I'll wear that.
Mother: I washed it yesterday. You can wear your trousers tomorrow.

[pause]

Now listen again.

[repeat]

[pause]

Question 4   *Four. What homework is the girl doing now?*

Boy: Have you finished the science homework yet?
Girl: I'm still working on it. What are you doing?
Boy: I've done my maths and I've just started those English exercises.
Girl: I'm going to do them next.

[pause]

Now listen again.

[repeat]

[pause]

Question 5   *Five. What's David going to buy?*

David: I'm just going to the shops, Mum. Do you need anything?
Mother: Yes, get some fruit will you – some green cooking apples and some oranges to make juice with.
David: Well, we already have lots of oranges.
Mother: OK, just some apples then. I'll make the juice when you get back.

[pause]

Now listen again.

[repeat]

[pause]

This is the end of Part One. Now look at Part Two.

[pause]

PART 2   *Listen to Sonya talking to Martin about her family.*
How old are her brothers and sisters?
For questions 6 to 10, write a letter, A to H, next to each person.
You will hear the conversation twice.

[pause]

Martin: You've got a big family, Sonya, haven't you?
Sonya: Well, Martin, there are six children altogether and I'm twenty and the oldest.
Martin: Wow! I know Vivienne, of course. She had her fifteenth birthday last month, didn't she?

Sonya:	That was Sally. Vivienne looks older but she's two years younger – but you mustn't say I told you she's only thirteen!
Martin:	Of course I won't. Well, my little sister's seven …
Sonya:	… and she plays with my brother Roger.
Martin:	So they must be the same age.
Sonya:	They are. Then there's my other little brother, Frank.
Martin:	And how old is he?
Sonya:	He's two years younger than Roger.
Martin:	So he's only five. There must be someone else.
Sonya:	… Oh, Deborah! I nearly forgot.
Martin:	Isn't she eighteen and starting at college in September?
Sonya:	Yes, she's going to study medicine. She's wanted to do that since she was ten.
Martin:	What a nice family.

[pause]

Now listen again.

[repeat]

[pause]

This is the end of Part Two. Now look at Part Three.

[pause]

PART 3   *Listen to a woman asking a travel agent for some information about a park in the mountains.*
For questions 11 to 15, tick A, B or C. You will hear the conversation twice.
Look at questions 11 to 15 now. You have 20 seconds.

[pause]

Now listen to the conversation.

Man:	Can I help you?
Woman:	I'd like some information about the mountain park. I've got seven days' holiday next month.
Man:	Yes, certainly.
Woman:	First, I'd like to book somewhere to stay.
Man:	I'm afraid there's nothing in the park, just a small café, that's all. The nearest guest-house is in a village a few kilometres away.
Woman:	Has the village got somewhere to swim or a cinema?
Man:	It's very quiet. There's just a small supermarket that sells food.
Woman:	I don't mind that. Can I take my car to the park?
Man:	Yes. But you must leave it at the entrance with the other cars and buses. Visitors must walk through the park.
Woman:	And how much does it cost to go in?
Man:	From Mondays to Fridays everyone pays twelve dollars, but at weekends it's thirteen dollars for children and sixteen dollars for adults.
Woman:	Right. Will I see any animals in the park next month?
Man:	I don't think so. But it's the best time to go! There won't be any snow and the flowers will be beautiful.

[pause]

Now listen again.

[repeat]

[pause]

This is the end of Part Three. Now look at Part Four.

[pause]

PART 4   *You will hear Mats talking to his friend, Sarah, about a trip to Manchester in England.*
Listen and complete questions 16 to 20. You will hear the conversation twice.

[pause]

Sarah:	Hello.
Mats:	Hello, Sarah. It's Mats.
Sarah:	Hi, Mats! How are you? Are you going to come to England in October?
Mats:	Yes, I am. I'm really happy. I'm going to visit Manchester. That's why I'm phoning. I have some questions.
Sarah:	What do you need to know?
Mats:	First, what will the weather be like? Will it be cold?
Sarah:	Well, it'll be autumn – the temperature will be 14 degrees.
Mats:	So, what clothes shall I bring?
Sarah:	Well, it rains a lot in Manchester, so bring a raincoat.
Mats:	OK. Next question. How do I get to Manchester from Heathrow Airport?
Sarah:	You can take the underground into the centre of London and then a train from Euston station. That's E-U-S-T-O-N. And there's also a plane from Heathrow to Manchester.
Mats:	Which is the cheaper?
Sarah:	The train, I think. It's £30.
Mats:	And finally, can I bring you anything from my country, Sarah?
Sarah:	Oh, yes, please! Can you bring me some cheese? I always like food.
Mats:	No problem. See you in October.
Sarah:	Bye!

[pause]

Now listen again.

[repeat]

[pause]

This is the end of Part Four. Now look at Part Five.

[pause]

PART 5   *You will hear some information about a museum.*
Listen and complete questions 21 to 25. You will hear the information twice.

[pause]

Man:	The Redfern Museum is closed today. Our opening hours are from half past one to half past four Monday to Thursday.

The museum has things for you to see from the eighteenth century – the downstairs room shows the clothes of two hundred years ago. For example, you can see what children wore at school and what families wore for dinner.

Upstairs, we are showing some important paintings by Spanish artists of the time. There's a short film about this exhibition every afternoon and there will be talks about some of these pictures in November.

In the Garden Room, there will be free concerts all through December for visitors to the museum. A ticket to the museum costs five pounds for adults, three pounds eighty for students and two pounds fifty for children.

We welcome school group visits. Please phone our Schools Officer for further information on double five seven six four two, between nine and five every day.

Come to Redfern Museum soon. Thank you for calling.

[pause]

Now listen again.

[repeat]

[pause]

This is the end of Part Five.

You now have eight minutes to write your answers on the answer sheet.

Note: Teacher, stop the recording here and time eight minutes. Remind the students when there is **one** minute remaining.

[pause]

This is the end of the test.

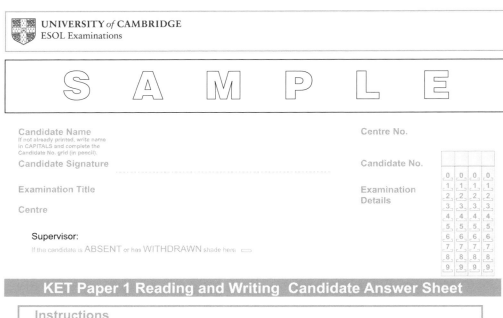

Part 1

1	A	B	C	D	E	F	G	H
2	A	B	C	D	E	F	G	H
3	A	B	C	D	E	F	G	H
4	A	B	C	D	E	F	G	H
5	A	B	C	D	E	F	G	H

Part 2

6	A	B	C
7	A	B	C
8	A	B	C
9	A	B	C
10	A	B	C

Part 3

11	A	B	C	16	A	B	C	D E F G H
12	A	B	C	17	A	B	C	D E F G H
13	A	B	C	18	A	B	C	D E F G H
14	A	B	C	19	A	B	C	D E F G H
15	A	B	C	20	A	B	C	D E F G H

Part 4

21	A	B	C
22	A	B	C
23	A	B	C
24	A	B	C
25	A	B	C
26	A	B	C
27	A	B	C

Part 5

28	A	B	C
29	A	B	C
30	A	B	C
31	A	B	C
32	A	B	C
33	A	B	C
34	A	B	C
35	A	B	C

Turn over for
Parts 6 - 9 →

Sample answer sheet – Reading and Writing (Sheet 2)

For **Parts 6, 7 and 8:**

Write your answers in the spaces next to the numbers (36 to 55) like this:

0	example

Part 6	Do not write here
36	1 36 0
37	1 37 0
38	1 38 0
39	1 39 0
40	1 40 0

Part 7	Do not write here
41	1 41 0
42	1 42 0
43	1 43 0
44	1 44 0
45	1 45 0
46	1 46 0
47	1 47 0
48	1 48 0
49	1 49 0
50	1 50 0

Part 8	Do not write here
51	1 51 0
52	1 52 0
53	1 53 0
54	1 54 0
55	1 55 0

Part 9 (Question 56): Write your answer below.

Do not write below (Examiner use only)
0   1   2   3   4   5

Sample answer sheet – Listening

S A M P L E

Candidate Name
If not already printed, write name
in CAPITALS and complete the
Candidate No. grid (in pencil).

Candidate Signature

Examination Title

Centre

Supervisor:
If the candidate is ABSENT or has WITHDRAWN shade here ▭

Centre No.

Candidate No.

Examination Details

0	0	0	0
1	1	1	1
2	2	2	2
3	3	3	3
4	4	4	4
5	5	5	5
6	6	6	6
7	7	7	7
8	8	8	8
9	9	9	9

KET Paper 2 Listening Candidate Answer Sheet

Instructions

Use a PENCIL (B or HB).

Rub out any answer you want to change with an eraser.

For **Parts 1, 2** and **3**:
Mark ONE letter for each question.
For example, if you think **C** is the right answer to the
question, mark your answer sheet like this:

0	A B C

Part 1	
1	A B C
2	A B C
3	A B C
4	A B C
5	A B C

Part 2	
6	A B C D E F G H
7	A B C D E F G H
8	A B C D E F G H
9	A B C D E F G H
10	A B C D E F G H

Part 3	
11	A B C
12	A B C
13	A B C
14	A B C
15	A B C

For **Parts 4** and **5**:
Write your answers in the spaces next to the
numbers (16 to 25) like this:

0	example

Part 4		Do not write here
16		1 16 0
17		1 17 0
18		1 18 0
19		1 19 0
20		1 20 0

Part 5		Do not write here
21		1 21 0
22		1 22 0
23		1 23 0
24		1 24 0
25		1 25 0